"I am grateful for Johnson's wise, sensitive, and practical insights for the local church committed to going global. While written by a North American, this book is neither culturally bound nor ethnocentrically blind. The issues addressed apply to any healthy local church anywhere in the world. In other words, *Missions* is thoroughly biblical. And for this reason, those like me who minister in another culture will find its lessons doable. I heartily recommend it, praying that God will grant it a wide readership, for his global glory."

Doug Van Meter, pastor-teacher, Brackenhurst Baptist Church, Johannesburg, South Africa

"I love this book. I love the way it begins and ends with the glory of God in the gospel. I love the way it places the local church at the center of both sending missionaries and the task of mission. I love the way it's driven by biblical principles yet full of practical advice. All the ingredients are here to transform the place of world missions in your congregation. World mission is our responsibility, your responsibility."

Tim Chester, pastor, Grace Church, Boroughbridge, United Kingdom; faculty member, Crosslands; author, *Good News to the Poor* and *Mission Matters*

"Johnson has given the church a gift in this practical guidebook for launching, sending, and sustaining missional endeavors in your local church. Every believer should read this book!"

Robby Gallaty, lead pastor, Long Hollow Baptist Church, Hendersonville, Tennessee

"In an increasingly post-Christian society, you may feel the mission pinch. How can we give our time, energy, attention, finances, and personnel to global missions when the needs are so great, and growing, here at home? If you feel buried in local needs, this short book may be exactly what you need to lift your head to God's international work and glory, open your eyes to the global cause in which we minister, and expand your heart to be more like his. Perhaps what your busy and bruised church needs is precisely a vision and passion for what God is up to around the world and not just around the corner. Cultivating a heart for God's global glory and sending our best people and resources into his cause will not detract from ~~ministry~~ l and real."

David Mathis, exec s Church, Minneapolis, Minne s *through the Spiritual Discipli*

D1393385

"Andy Johnson has given us a doctrinally sound yet highly practical blueprint to guide the local church in going global in the twenty-first century. I pray that this volume will be widely circulated among pastors and lay leaders."

Al Jackson, pastor, Lakeview Baptist Church, Auburn, Alabama

"As a pastor, I could not be more thankful for this book by Andy Johnson. Although books on missions abound, this one fills a void felt by any local church trying to discern how best to be involved in taking the gospel to the nations. Not only does it lay a much-needed foundation and framework for missions; it also answers the practical questions that inevitably arise. Both challenging and helpful, particularly for local church leaders, it is the book I've been looking for since I first began my pastoral ministry. I will make it available and encourage every member to read it."

J. Josh Smith, lead pastor, MacArthur Blvd. Baptist Church, Irving, Texas

"A seasoned missions pastor, Johnson gives insightful, practical guidance to help churches reshape their missions strategies more biblically and faithfully. Especially valuable is his emphasis on the role of the local church, too often underplayed in missions circles today. I will eagerly hand this book out to all our church leaders and missionaries."

John Folmar, senior pastor, United Christian Church of Dubai

"The church has been tasked with the mission of making disciples of all nations. Too often the local church is pulled in several directions without a clear guiding vision for its mission efforts. As a pastor, I am grateful for Andy Johnson's book because it helps church leaders to develop a plan for their mission pursuits that is well-intentioned instead of ambiguous and proactive instead of reactionary. I highly recommend this book to all church leaders who desire a well-thought-out vision for engaging the nations with the gospel."

Afshin Ziafat, lead pastor, Providence Church, Frisco, Texas

"In *Missions*, Andy Johnson argues that the church glorifies God not only in working to gather true worshipers from all peoples, but also in using the means he has outlined in Scriptures to fulfill those ends. Because there is much debate about what missions is, how to do missions, and who is a missionary, Johnson spends a great part of the book helping us find answers that are rooted in scriptural commands, examples, and principles. If you desire to do missions in a way that only God gets the glory, you'll want to read this book and pass it around to others who love God and love to see unbelieving people become followers of Jesus Christ."

Juan R. Sanchez, senior pastor, High Pointe Baptist Church, Austin, Texas; author, *1 Peter for You*

MISSIONS

9Marks: Building Healthy Churches

Edited by Mark Dever and Jonathan Leeman

BUILDING HEALTHY CHURCHES

MISSIONS

HOW
THE LOCAL
CHURCH GOES
GLOBAL

ANDY JOHNSON
Foreword by David Platt

Missions: How the Local Church Goes Global

Copyright © 2017 by Andy Johnson

Published by Crossway, a publishing ministry of Good News Publishers, Wheaton, Illinois 60187, U.S.A

This edition published by arrangement with Crossway. All rights reserved. This edition published in Great Britain in 2018.

The right of Andy Johnson to be identified as the Author of this Work has been asserted by him in accordance with the Copyright, Designs and Patents Act 1988.

British Library Cataloguing in Publication Data

A record for this book is available from the British Library

Cover design: Darren Welch Illustration by Wayne Brezinka

Unless otherwise indicated, Scripture quotations are from the ESV® Bible (The Holy Bible, English Standard Version®), copyright © 2001 by Crossway, a publishing minis- try of Good News Publishers. Used by permission. All rights reserved.

Scripture references marked NIV are taken from The Holy Bible, New International Version®, NIV®. Copyright © 1973, 1978, 1984, 2011 by Biblica, Inc.TM Used by permis- sion. All rights reserved worldwide.

ISBN: 978-1-912373-20-8

Printed in Denmark by Nørhaven

10Publishing, a division of 10ofthose.com
Unit C, Tomlinson Road, Leyland, PR25 2DY, England

Email: info@10ofthose.com
Website: www.10ofthose.com

To my wife, Rebecca,
my best earthly partner in our joyful labor for
the spread of the gospel to all peoples

Answers can be given solely on the basis of Scripture. For the work of missions is the work of God; it is not lawful for us to improvise.

J. H. Bavinck, veteran missionary to Indonesia[1]

CONTENTS

SERIES PREFACE

Do you believe it's your responsibility to help build a healthy church? If you are a Christian, we believe that it is.

Jesus commands you to make disciples (Matt. 28:18–20). Jude says to build yourselves up in the faith (Jude 20–21). Peter calls you to use your gifts to serve others (1 Pet. 4:10). Paul tells you to speak the truth in love so that your church will become mature (Eph. 4:13, 15). Do you see where we are getting this?

Whether you are a church member or leader, the Building Healthy Churches series of books aims to help you fulfill such biblical commands and so play your part in building a healthy church. Another way to say it might be, we hope these books will help you grow in loving your church like Jesus loves your church.

9Marks plans to produce a short, readable book on each of what Mark has called nine marks of a healthy church, plus one more on sound doctrine. Watch for books on expositional preaching, biblical theology, the gospel, conversion, evange-lism, church membership, church discipline, discipleship and growth, and church leadership.

Local churches exist to display God's glory to the nations. We do that by fixing our eyes on the gospel of Jesus Christ, trusting him for salvation, and then loving one another with

God's own holiness, unity, and love. We pray the book you are holding will help.

With hope,
Mark Dever and Jonathan Leeman
series editors

FOREWORD

Over a hundred years ago, George Pentecost said, "To the pastor belongs the privilege and responsibility of solving the foreign missionary problem."[1] Pentecost maintained that mission boards play important roles in missions: devising methods, fueling movements, and raising money. But it is the responsibility and privilege of pastors to feel the weight of the nations and to fan a flame for the global glory of God in every local church.

I believe he was right.

Let me be clear that I am *not* saying pastors should neglect ministry to people in our local churches. I know there are people in our churches who are hurting, whose marriages are struggling, whose children are rebelling, and who are walking through cancer and tumors and all sorts of other challenges in this life. We should not neglect local ministry to the body of Christ.

Nor should we neglect local mission in our communities or cities. We have been commanded to make disciples, and that command will most naturally and consistently play out right where we live, in the context of our immediate surroundings. Every church member ought to ask, "With the unique gifts God has given me and the Spirit of God who lives in me, how can I make disciples today right where I live?" In this way, there ought to be disciple-making and church-planting efforts where we live and across North America. Local mission is totally necessary.

At the same time, global missions is tragically neglected.

I was near Yemen not long ago. Northern Yemen has approximately eight million people. Do you know how many believers there are in northern Yemen? Twenty or thirty. Out of eight million people—the populations of Alabama and Mississippi combined. There are likely more believers in your Sunday school class or a couple of small groups in your church than there are in all of northern Yemen. That is a problem. It's a problem because millions of people in the northern part of Yemen have no access to the gospel. They join millions and millions of other unreached people in the world who are born, live, and die without ever even hearing the good news of what God has done for their salvation in Christ.

It's not primarily the job of missions organizations to address that problem. This is primarily the job of every local church. Specifically, it's the primary responsibility of every pastor of every local church to love people in that church and to love people in that community, all toward the ultimate end that the name of Christ might be praised among every group of people on the planet. That's what the Spirit of Christ wants, so that's what every Christian, every pastor, and every local church should want.

When we read through the book of Acts, we see a clear priority within the roles of the local church: the priority of spreading the gospel across the globe. In Acts 13, we see the church at Antioch worshiping, fasting, and praying, and in the context of that local church with its leaders, the Spirit sets apart Paul and Barnabas as missionaries. The church prays over them and sends them out, supporting them as they go. Twice Paul returns to Antioch to encourage that local church, and then on his third missionary journey, he writes a letter to another local church, at Rome, to ask for their support in helping him get to Spain, where Christ has not yet been named. In this way, we see local churches sending, shepherding, and supporting men and women on global missions.

For this reason, I want to encourage every pastor and every leader of every local church to take up this mantle of global missions—to see the unique Antioch-type role God has given you and your church in the spread of the gospel to the ends of the earth. But you may wonder, "Where do I begin?"

That is why I am so grateful for the simple, significant book you hold in your hands. Andy Johnson has done a great service to local churches and global missions in the pages that lie ahead. Grounded in God's Word from start to finish, this book draws from experience in both the church where Andy serves and churches across the world he has worked alongside. As a result, it offers a treasure trove of wisdom available to leaders and members in churches of all sizes. After I finished reading this book, I thought, "I wish every pastor and leader of every local church could read this!" For if they did, I am convinced it would radically change not only the shape of local churches in our communities but also the cause of global missions in the world.

For this reason, I wholeheartedly commend this book to you, prayerful that God might use it to fan a flame for his global glory in your life and your local church.

David Platt

INTRODUCTION

Missions at a Crossroad

Beth stopped for a drive-through espresso on her way home from the church missions committee meeting. She hoped a shot of industrial-strength caffeine might tone down the head-ache throbbing in her temples. While she waited, she kept re-playing the meeting in her mind. Everyone on the committee seemed to love Jesus and care about missions. So why were their meetings so frustrating? Another evening had been spent in misunderstanding and cross-purposes, with nothing finally accomplished. Despite their obvious concern for "missions," Beth was beginning to wonder if they actually meant the same thing by that word.

Dave began the meeting chastising the committee for its "myopic" focus on evangelism. "What about the poor, the hungry, the oppressed?" he asked. "Isn't it the mission of the church to care for all their physical needs too?"

And Olivia again suggested it would be so much better (and cheaper) to pay local pastors than to send out Western missionaries.

Then there was Harold's comment. He had just read some

17

study describing a new method that some missionary organization used to produce "87 percent more decisions for Christ among Muslims" than merely preaching the gospel from the Bible. Was a statistical study really the best way to decide what methods to employ? And what exactly were those Muslims deciding?

Patricia pressured the committee to stop supporting full-time missionaries altogether and instead focus on sending people overseas with their jobs. "The old model of churches sending supported long-term workers is just outdated in our modern, global economy," she asserted. "Business as missions is the only way to go." Beth agreed this could be a good thing to encourage, but she was pretty confident the apostle John's command that we "ought to support" church-sent missionaries "that we may be fellow workers for the truth" still applied (3 John 8). But when Beth read that passage out loud, Patricia just rolled her eyes and encouraged her to stop looking backward and embrace the next wave of missions.

And, of course, Clarence concluded the meeting by encouraging them (again) to focus more on short-term trips rather than funding more long-term workers. "Short-term trips can be life changing for our people," he reminded them, just before launching into the familiar story about his trip to paint a community center in Guatemala and how it had transformed his faith. But Beth wondered if those kinds of trips were really the best use of their missions funds and a missionary's time.

The click of the drive-through window startled Beth out of her reflections. As she drove away nursing her double shot, she had a growing sense that there must be a better way. Surely

God must have given more direction about what the mission is and how we should pursue it. But she couldn't think of where to find that direction or where to start.

Sadly, I don't think Beth is alone.

In many of our churches today, well-meaning people seem to struggle with the concept of missions. They want to see Christ glorified and honored. They care about the needs of people. But in practice their pursuit of missions often devolves into a frantic hunt for new ideas, competition over church resources, and disagreements over method.

The good news of this little book is that it doesn't have to be that way.

Imagine a local church where the congregation's mission to the nations is clear and agreed upon. Elders guide the congregation toward strategic missions. Missions is held up as a concern for all Christians, not just the niche "missions club." The tyranny of new trends and demands for immediate, visible results holds no sway. Members see missions as the work of the church together rather than the personal, private activity of the individual. In this church, members see missions as a core ministry of the church, not an occasional short-term project. Relationships with missionaries are deep, serious, and lasting. Joyful giving to missions is a basic part of the church's budget, not merely the fruit of occasional and desperate appeals. And members actually value missions enough that some want to uproot their lives and be sent out long-term by the church.

This isn't an impractical idea, nor an especially complicated project to realize. I've seen this vision become a reality in numerous churches, large and small. It's not that hard. It all flows primarily from finding one's missions agenda and methods in the Bible.

That's the main premise of this book: God's Word gives us everything we need to know to obey him and bring him glory. That includes everything we need in order to obey his Great Commission to make disciples among all nations (Matt. 28:18–20). That doesn't mean his Word explicitly addresses every question we might invent. Nor that every suggestion in this book comes directly from a biblical command or example. But it does mean that the Bible is fully sufficient to give us the agenda and principles that inform our methods and decisions. In it we find a wealth of principles and imperatives that will give order and shape to our endeavors, and in the process free us from the oppressive tyranny that comes from relying only on our own pragmatic resources and humanly devised notions.

One of the things we see clearly in Scripture is that a concern for missions is for all Christians, because it is a concern for every local church, together. So whether you are an interested church member, a missions leader, or a local church pastor, this book has something in it for you.

But before we can discuss the work of missions, we first need to nail down a few foundational biblical principles. Then we can consider how we might apply them with wisdom to our own missions activities. So let's get started at the place where all wise Christian endeavors should start—with the Bible.

1

A BIBLICAL FOUNDATION FOR MISSIONS

I once rented a vacation apartment on the sixth floor of a building with no elevator. The owner had been very clear in every email, stating, "This apartment is on the sixth floor and there is no elevator." Still, the significance of her disclosure didn't really hit me until I was panting on the fifth-floor landing, hauling suitcase number two of three up the winding stairs. Yet, as I stood there trying to remember the symptoms of a heart attack, I couldn't feel angry toward the owner. She had been up-front about it, all along. I should have paid more attention.

Full disclosure is a good and honest way to begin any relationship, including the relationship between a writer (like me) and a reader (like you). That's why I want to begin this book by stating some foundational biblical convictions about missions. You may not agree with each and every one of them. I hope you won't put this book down if you don't. There might be useful stuff here, even if we don't agree on everything. And then you, as a reader, can be like the Bereans in Acts 17 and test everything to see if it squares with the Bible.

We need to start by defining the aim of the church's mission.

THE MISSION OF MISSIONS IS PRIMARILY SPIRITUAL

At the outset of a small book we don't need to enter deeply into the debate about churches' responsibility to meet both eternal needs through gospel proclamation *and* temporal needs through material care. Christians as individuals clearly should care about all human suffering. And Christians should especially care about the terrible, eternal suffering facing all those who remain under God's wrath. We needn't pit the two concerns against one another in our personal lives. John Piper has balanced it well, saying: "Christians care about all suffering, especially eternal suffering. Else they have a defective heart or a flameless hell."[1]

As we turn to the global mission of the church, I hope we can agree that the church should especially care about eternal suffering. The church is that unique gospel community chartered by Jesus Christ himself. Consequently, it should especially labor to fulfill its unique mission to guard the gospel, proclaim the gospel, and disciple those who respond in repentance and faith to the gospel. If our churches fail at that mission, no matter what other good things we do, we will have failed in the unique mandate that Christ has given us as churches. It is good to do other good things, and our churches may make different decisions about engaging in good works and social action. But it is the stewardship of the gospel that remains utterly unique to the Christian church. We must keep first things first. That is the priority of Christian missions.

It's important to press this point right up front because in recent days some Christians have suggested that encouraging churches to prioritize a spiritual mission means their members and missionaries won't care at all about earthly human suffering. Historically, though, it has often been the generations whose churches focused most on heaven and salvation that have done the most social good. Even today researchers like Robert Putnam puzzle over the unusual level of altruistic giving by religious people from heavenly minded churches.[2] Or we might read the widely acclaimed work of sociologist Robert Woodberry, who demonstrated that "conversionary missionary protestants" (meaning missionaries who prioritize saving souls above all else) have done more lasting social good globally than those who only, or mainly, focus on doing social good alone.[3]

Of course, at the end of the day we don't prioritize eternal matters in our churches because of history or social science. We do it for love of neighbor. If we are convinced that eternal suffering in hell is the most pernicious of all human suffering, what else would we prioritize? Even more, we prioritize eternal matters for love of God. We want our churches to fulfill the God-glorifying purpose for which he specially entrusted them with the gospel in the first place.

We are joyfully driven by the command of our Lord to "make disciples of all nations, baptizing them in the name of the Father and of the Son and of the Holy Spirit, teaching them to observe all that I have commanded you" (Matt. 28:19–20). And we are driven by the apostle John's heavenly vision:

> After this I looked, and behold, a great multitude that no one could number, from every nation, from all tribes and peoples and languages, standing before the throne and before the Lamb, clothed in white robes, with palm branches in their hands, crying out with a loud voice, "Salvation belongs to our God who sits on the throne, and to the Lamb!" (Rev. 7:9–10)

Calling and discipling all the peoples saved by the Lamb is the primary mission of missions. Whatever other good things a church may choose to do, that great vision must be our most fundamental objective and the joy toward which we labor. Would anything less be worthy of the one who "came into the world to save sinners" (1 Tim. 1:15)? Evangelism and establishing Christ's church is our first priority in missions.

THE MISSION BELONGS TO GOD, FOR HIS GLORY, ON HIS TERMS

God intends not only that his mission would go forward but that it would go forward on his terms. He means to get glory by showing that the mission is his and that his power sustains it. Any effort on our part to change or broaden the mission, or to substitute our ideas for God's, runs the risk of trying to rob God of his rightful glory. And trying to rob an all-knowing and all-powerful God of the thing he is most passionate about in all the universe is breathtakingly stupid and ultimately pointless. God says:

> For my name's sake I defer my anger;
>> for the sake of my praise I restrain it for you,
>> that I may not cut you off.

Behold, I have refined you, but not as silver;
    I have tried you in the furnace of affliction.
For my own sake, for my own sake, I do it,
    for how should my name be profaned?
My glory I will not give to another. (Isa. 48:9–11)

God cares about how the mission goes forward because he will not give his glory to another. As we look to the pages of Scripture to understand the mission, this fact must remain etched in our minds. The mission of global redemption is ultimately for God's sake: "For my own sake, for my own sake, I do it." And that is a wonderful thing.

Our confidence in missions and our joy in salvation flow from a knowledge that God's mission of mercy finds its origin in his desire for his glory, not in our ability or desirability. Praise God! God declares,

For my name's sake I defer my anger;
    for the sake of my praise I restrain it for you,
    that I may not cut you off.

That may be one of the most encouraging verses in all of Scripture. As long as God cares about his own glory, and as long as he remains committed to getting glory by showing mercy to sinners, all those who trust in him are secure, and his mission will never fail. God has decided how the mission should go forward. He intends it to go forward by the simple declaration of the gospel and the gathering of his children into churches, so that everyone will see that salvation is God's work, and he will get all the glory.

GLOBAL MISSIONS IS PRIMARILY THROUGH THE LOCAL CHURCH

Who is responsible to carry out this mission of global salvation? To whom did Christ give his Great Commission in Matthew 28? That's a more complicated question than merely asking who was there when he spoke the words recorded in Matthew 28:18–20. In one sense the commission to missions was given to every individual Christian. But in another sense it was given primarily to local churches. Why would I say that?

Each of us individually is called to obey Christ's command to make disciples who know and obey his Word. But how does he intend us to do that? His Word is clear—normally we are to pursue obedience, build up disciples, and plant other churches through the local church. The local church makes clear who is and who is not a disciple through baptism and membership in the body (Acts 2:41). The local church is where most discipling naturally takes place (Heb. 10:24–25). The local church sends out missionaries (Acts 13:3) and cares for missionaries after they are sent (Phil. 4:15–16; 3 John 1–8). And healthy, reproducing local churches are normally the aim and end of our missionary effort (Acts 15:41; Titus 1:5).

But why is God so committed to accomplishing this great work of redemption through his church? Because he is passionate for his own glory. He has determined to act through history "so that through the church the manifold wisdom of God might now be made known to the rulers and authorities in the heavenly places" (Eph. 3:10). God is committed to using the church to accomplish his work of redemption to display the glory of his wisdom to the universe. The church was God's idea. It is his one and only organizational plan for world missions. Most of all, it is his beloved Son's beloved, blood-bought bride.

Consequently, any humanly invented organizations that assist in missions must remember that they are the bridesmaids, not the bride. They are stagehands, not the star. That position and honor and responsibility has been given by Christ to his church, and only to his church. Organized cooperation among churches for the sake of missions is a wonderful thing (more on that later), but those who organize that cooperation must remember that they are coming alongside— not supplanting—the local church.

It's because the Bible is so clear on this point that this little book is so unapologetically focused on the local church as the engine of world missions. Even as we consider our own individual commitment to the global mission, we should do so in the context of our roles as church members. If we are to understand how to pursue the mission faithfully, the local church must be central to identifying, training, sending, and supporting. The mission has been given to Christ's church for Christ's glory.

THE BIBLE SAYS A LOT ABOUT HOW TO APPROACH MISSIONS

But how does God want his mission to go forward? It would be cruel for God to know what he wants, but then leave us to figure it all out. God would never treat his children that way. Throughout his Word, God has given us a treasury of instructions on the global mission of the church—what it is and how to approach the mission in faithfulness and joyful confidence.

We love and honor him not merely by working toward the final goal he's given—worshipers from every language, tribe, people, and nation—but also by using the means he has decreed. And he has told us that his global mission will advance through holy lives, faithful prayer, gospel proclamation, and healthy reproducing churches.

That's really what the rest of this book is about: unpacking these principles from the Bible and then trying to apply them with wisdom to the missionary practice of our local churches. Because the happy news is that though the work of global evangelism is difficult, it is not complicated. God has told us everything we must know right there in the Bible.

The Bible tells us what the mission is: the church's mission is to display the glory of God by declaring the gospel to all peoples, by gathering churches in every place, and by filling them with disciples who obey God and will praise him forever for his grace (Isaiah 56; Matt. 28:18–20; Rom. 15:7–13; Eph. 3:8–11; Rev. 7:9–10).

The Bible tells us how the mission will go forward: through prayerful dependence, gospel proclamation, biblical discipling, and church planting (Ex. 6:5–8; Rom. 10:17; Col. 4:2–4; 1 Thess. 5:11).

The Bible tells us what kind of missionaries we should support: biblically faithful, methodologically patient, gospel-proclaiming, church-loving missionaries (Acts 16:1–3; Rom. 10:14–15; 2 Cor. 8:23; 2 Tim. 4:1–5; 3 John 1–8).

The Bible tells us what the end goal of missions should be: transformed individuals in biblical churches who will ultimately join a heavenly multitude praising the Lamb of God forever (Rom. 8:1–11; Heb. 10:19–25; Rev. 7:9–10).

That's just a tiny sampling of what Scripture has to tell us about missions. We are not left alone to lean on our own puny resources to figure out the mission of the church for the nations. God is much too kind and serious to have done that. So let's move forward with these four biblical principles firmly in mind:

- The mission of missions is primarily spiritual.
- The mission belongs to God, for his glory, on his terms.
- God gave the mission to the local church.
- And the Bible tells us all we must know to faithfully fulfill God's mission.

With these principles clearly stated, let's begin to unpack and apply them.

2

FIRST THINGS FIRST

I remember the first time I rented a car while briefly living in Turkey. My in-laws were visiting, and my wife and I wanted to drive them to the ruins of Ephesus. The rental company gave us an upgrade to a new and very expensive European sedan. Excellent! Everything was going great, until I pulled into a gas station. The car clearly ran on gasoline. However, the pump attendant asked if I wanted "benzin" or "motorin." Somehow fuel vocabulary hadn't made it into my language lessons. For a moment I actually considered just picking one and hoping for the best. We needed to get going. Then I had a vision of what the wrong fuel might do to a car worth most of a year's salary. So began a five-minute round of hand gestures, nozzle sniffing, and finally Turkish dictionary consultations. It turns out that Turks call gasoline "benzin" and diesel oil "motorin." The attendant was highly amused at my expense. But I had to be sure, because no matter how good the car, or my intentions, trying to run it on the wrong fuel would not have been pretty.

I wonder if many churches need a similar lesson when it comes to fueling their passion for missions. The right fuel is the critical first step. Sadly, sometimes we're in too big a hurry, and so we use the wrong fuel. We give our time to world maps, demographics, and stories of missionary sacrifice. Or we contemplate the neediness of the lost, which is useful, but not as a point of initial departure. The heart for God-glorifying missions starts with joy in the gospel. Our churches must first cherish the God who sent his own Son to save sinners like us. The right fuel matters.

What this may mean is that the best way to encourage your church in missions is to stop talking about missions for a time and, instead, talk more about the gospel. I've seen churches that have tried to get their members excited about missions without being excited about the gospel. The result was pitiful. Missions became just one more ministry area competing for everyone's attention and interest. Guilt, hype, sad stories— none of them motivate in the best way. How do you really sell sacrifice (which is what missions involves) unless the people value supremely the thing for which the sacrifice is made? Do not try to get your church excited about missions until they love and value (really, deeply value) what Christ has done for them in the gospel. Churches won't extend themselves to commend the gospel until they deeply cherish the gospel.

WHAT IS THE GOSPEL?

What do I mean by "the gospel"? I mean the historic Christian message, the good news about what God has done for sinners through Christ. I do not mean the many implications of that message, including what Christians might do or how they might live. I'm talking about the message itself of what Jesus has done for sinners, the only message that can save sinners like us from hell and bring us to God.

The biblical gospel begins with God, who created all things by his word. Out of nothing God spoke into existence all the galaxies and nebulae, all the stars and every planet. On our planet he created life, including the first man and woman. God placed them in a garden and gave them everything to enjoy and to rule in perfect freedom. The only restriction was that they were not to eat from one particular tree. But God's rebellious enemy entered the garden and tempted the woman, Eve. The man, Adam, stood right there doing nothing. They chose to disbelieve God's instruction and instead listened to Satan's false promises. Humans have been doing the same thing ever since. Since God is good and just, he will punish sin. He's not the kind of judge that sweeps wrongs under the rug, perverting justice. He is a righteous judge. That's bad news for guilty lawbreakers like us.

Rebelling against the loving rule of a perfect God is unimaginably bad and deserves a punishment of unimaginable severity and duration. We deserve eternal, conscious punishment under God's wrath in hell.

But God, in his incalculable love and wisdom, had a plan to punish sin (and so be a just judge) and yet forgive sinners like us (and so display his mercy). He did that by sending Jesus, the coequal and coeternal Son of God, to take on human flesh. Jesus lived a perfect life without any rebellion against God. Jesus had no sins of his own but voluntarily stood in the place of sinners. Being nailed to a wooden cross, he bore the full force of the wrath of an all-powerful God's justified hatred of

33

sin. What our sin deserved for all eternity Christ took upon himself in loving agony. His self-sacrifice absorbed the punishment due to every sinner who would ever turn and trust in him. God showed his acceptance of Christ's sacrifice by raising Jesus from the dead after three days in the grave.

Now this risen Jesus commands everyone everywhere to turn away from sin and trust in him. And, amazingly, Christ holds out to us not only the promise of forgiveness but also adoption as loved sons and daughters of the very God we've offended. By repenting of our sin and trusting in Christ, we can know peace with God now and the secure hope of eternal joy with him forever. That is the biblical gospel. It's true for every person, in every language, in every place, in every culture, through all of time.

Regardless of our role in a church, the best thing we can do is to believe this gospel. We should reflect on it and measure everything in our lives in light of its truth and worth. Having done that, we should pray for our church leaders and gently encourage them to lead in holding up the gospel. Thank them every time they make the gospel clear in their preaching, and encourage them to see a passion for global missions as a natural biblical implication of the gospel.

If you are a pastor or church leader, this means you need to hold up this gospel not just in evangelistic appeals, but all the time. The saved people in your church gatherings need to be reminded regularly and helped to marvel at the idea that "while we were still sinners, Christ died for us" (Rom. 5:8). Where people see the work of Christ as supremely valuable, missions becomes a glorious and sensible sacrifice. The glory of the gospel—not the neediness of mankind—is the self-sustaining fuel for global missions.

WHAT DO "MISSIONS" AND "MISSIONARY" MEAN?

However, what do we mean by "missions," and who should be called a "missionary"? The two terms have gotten pretty significant makeovers in the minds of some Christians recently. Some now treat the mission of the church as encompassing every good thing a Christian might do, from social action to environmental protection. Those are certainly good things to do, along with the myriad other good things most Christians regularly do individually. For this book, though, I intend to stick to the traditional and historic use of "missions," meaning the unique, deliberate gospel mission of the church to make disciples of all the nations. I mean evangelism that takes the gospel across ethnic, linguistic, and geographic boundaries, that gathers churches, and teaches them to obey everything Jesus commended. Frankly, to do otherwise risks rendering the term "missions" largely useless. As Stephen Neill famously said of this new redefinition of missions, "If everything is mission, then nothing is mission."[1]

In the same way, when I refer to a missionary, I don't mean any Christian who lives cross-culturally and shares the gospel. In chapter 7 I'll discuss the valuable contribution these other Christians can make to the work of missions. But just as not every church member who loves Christ is a "pastor/elder," and not every church member who talks about the Bible is a "teacher" in the sense of James 3:1, so not every cross-cultural gospel witness is a missionary in the sense we read about in

3 John or 1 Corinthians. So again, I'll stick with the historic, traditional understanding of a missionary as someone identified and sent out by local churches to make the gospel known and to gather, serve, and strengthen local churches across ethnic, linguistic, or geographic divides. Those are the ones our churches are told that we ought to support in places like 3 John.

But what does this biblical support look like? And how do we get started as a church?

3

SENDING AND SUPPORTING WELL

I have a friend who grew up as a missionary kid in Europe. He recently told me about a visit he and his family once made to a church while in the United States. He was probably nine years old at the time. Soon after his family's arrival one of the church members invited him to come get some toys and other things from their church's "missionary closet." As a young boy he was intrigued and excited. Then the church member opened the door to a large closet. It was brimming over with worn out clothes, obsolete computers, and cast off toys with missing parts. My friend was crushed.

I trust the folks at this church were well-meaning. But surely a closet of cast-off junk isn't God's ideal for missionary support. But what is his ideal? How do we send missionaries well, how much support is enough, and whom do we even send? No surprise, the answer is right there in the Bible.

BASIC PRINCIPLES FROM 3 JOHN 1–8
In his third letter, the apostle John instructs his friend Gaius about the importance of supporting itinerate missionary

evangelists. In the process, he gives us a number of biblical principles to shape the way we think about our own missionary sending and support.

Calling himself "the elder," John writes:

> The elder to the beloved Gaius, whom I love in truth.
>
> Beloved, I pray that all may go well with you and that you may be in good health, as it goes well with your soul. For I rejoiced greatly when the brothers came and testified to your truth, as indeed you are walking in the truth. I have no greater joy than to hear that my children are walking in the truth.
>
> Beloved, it is a faithful thing you do in all your efforts for these brothers, strangers as they are, who testified to your love before the church. You will do well to send them on their journey in a manner worthy of God. For they have gone out for the sake of the name, accepting nothing from the Gentiles. Therefore we ought to support people like these, that we may be fellow workers for the truth. (3 John 1–8)

There are a number of direct implications for missions in this short passage. Let's consider five.

1. *Concern for missions and missionaries is normal (vv. 3, 5, 8).* John asserts that his friend Gaius is "walking in the truth," and that "it is a faithful thing you do in all your efforts for these brothers." He concludes that "we ought to support people like these [missionaries]." Scripture is clear that a desire to support the spread of the gospel to those who have not heard is a normal part of basic Christian health.

2. *Cooperation among local churches is encouraged (vv. 3, 7).* Likewise, cooperation in missions between multiple local congregations is taken for granted as a good thing. These gospel

workers went out from another church, likely John's. They were "strangers" to Gaius (v. 5), so clearly not from his congregation. And yet John says that Gaius "ought" to support these people so that together John's church and Gaius's church might partner together for the truth. Mutual support of missionaries is real gospel partnership that brings honor to Christ.

3. *Knowing whom we ought to support is crucial (vv. 6–8).* But how can we know whom to support? The apostle John narrows it down for us considerably. Certainly we hope Christians share the gospel as they scatter because of persecution (Acts 8:4) or travel in pursuit of business (James 4:13). But John describes a special moral obligation to support those who have been sent out "for the sake of the name." These are the ones to whom we "ought" to give material support. Despite globalization and mobility, until Christ returns, there will always be a need for churches to train, send, and financially support intentional missionaries. What's more, when John notes that these missionaries were "accepting nothing from the Gentiles," he seems to mean they were not earning money from the gospel; so the church should supply their needs. Lots of people share the gospel. Praise God! But only some have a moral claim on the local church's financial support. These are the men and women whom we call missionaries.

Missionaries are not just self-styled free agents. They should be accountable to a specific local church. The missionaries mentioned in 3 John are probably accountable to John's church in Ephesus. Did you notice the church connection in verse 6? John tells Gaius that these missionaries "testified to your love before the church." After having been supported by Gaius they returned to the church that sent them and re-ported back. John's letter, among other things, seems to be his church's commendation of these missionaries as their own ap-proved workers. Biblical missionaries are connected to a local church. It's always been that way.

4. *Support should be abundant (v. 6).* Likewise, John doesn't leave us to wonder what our support for missionaries should look like. It should be lavish, abundant, provided "in a manner worthy of God." This concern that Christian workers would be amply supplied is echoed elsewhere in the Bible. Paul instructs Titus, "Do your best to speed Zenas the lawyer and Apollos on their way; see that they lack nothing" (Titus 3:13). Our support for missionaries should aim to see that they lack nothing, as if we were supplying Jesus himself for a journey. It's a high bar.

5. *The motivation is love for the glory of Christ (vv. 7–8).* Finally, we see the motivation that should drive all this going and sending and supporting—love for the glory and knowledge of the name and truth of Christ. This is the engine of the mis-sionary enterprise—for the sake of Christ's name. The needs of those yet unreached by the gospel are great, but John presses us to send for the fame of Christ's great name and the glory of his truth.

These principles from 3 John are clear, and obedience to them might revolutionize how some of us think about sup-porting missions from our churches. How do we apply them?

ASSESSING WOULD-BE MISSIONARIES

Given the seriousness and obligations entailed in sending out missionaries, we should carefully select whom we would send and support. Concerns about giving missionaries too much may just show we have done a poor job vetting those we send. If we choose the right people, we need not worry about giving them too much money. I have known a number of faithful missionaries who found themselves "oversupplied." They simply put the money to other gospel uses. They bought Bibles; they paid to train local preachers; they funded gospel translation projects. To my knowledge, none of them spirited the funds to a secret bank account or bought an extravagant car. If you are seriously concerned that excess money given to your missionaries will be wasted, you should probably bring them home and send out trustworthy missionaries instead.

Yes, some caution is merited. Missionaries are fallen sinners saved by grace, just like the rest of us. But our responsibility is to send discerningly, not support suspiciously. Scripture is clear that not all who put themselves forward for Christian work are suitable. Later in 3 John we are introduced to Diotrephes. He put himself forward for leadership in the church, but John had nothing good to say about him. A desire to serve is not a sufficient qualification. In the same way, the self-appointed messengers in Acts 15 were not qualified merely because they wanted to go to Antioch. We as churches should be very careful about whom we might "lay hands on."

It is precisely for this reason that a too-narrow focus on the urgency of missions may be unhelpful. I have in mind sermons and slogans that emphasize the urgency of the missionary task above all else. God's mission *is* urgent. Hell is real and God's wrath is certain for all outside of Christ. Yet God's mission is not frantic or in danger of failing. The promise that

41

Christ will lose none of those the Father has given him is not standing on a knife's edge, with failure just a breath away. We can be both urgent *and* wise. Jesus told us to plead with the Lord of the harvest not for warm bodies but for "laborers" (Matt. 9:38; Luke 10:2). Those are the people we should send. Sending unqualified people may produce bad consequences that cascade far beyond the individual.

My father owned a small business when I was growing up. He was a good, wise, and godly man, but having spent his life working the ranches and oil fields of Texas, he was not an especially gentle person. He didn't suffer lightly the burden of lazy or disruptive employees. I once overheard Dad instructing one of his managers to dismiss a problem employee. My dad concluded by saying, "Whenever that man's here, it's like having two good men gone." The image has stuck with me. Sending the wrong people overseas isn't just poor stewardship. It can encumber the fruitfulness of other workers. We don't need missionaries whose effect is like two good missionaries gone.

Being wise about who we send begins with how we speak about missions. Have you ever heard someone say, "Christians don't need a reason to go; they need a reason to stay"? Such exhortations may not help as much as we think. True, missionaries are not the superelites of the Christian world. But is it really the best correction to imply that anyone without a good reason to stay is qualified to be a missionary? Of course not. Too often, I fear, church leaders encourage missionary zeal in people with questionable qualifications and then leave it to the "professionals" at a sending agency to have the hard conversations.

Instead, local churches should take a more active and

thoughtful role in encouraging and equipping members to go to the nations. I know some may think they lack the expertise to train up missionaries. But if you know how to train up healthy members in your own church, you actually do know most of what's needed to train up a missionary. Here are three things to assess.

Assess Character

First, who better than a local church to assess the character of would-be missionaries? So often missionaries work in contexts without regular daily oversight. Much of what they do is relational, unstructured, and self-initiated. We need to send people who are self-starters yet faithful and willing to submit to authority. As we talk with members of our churches about going to the nations, we—not some parachurch sending agency—should be the ones to evaluate their character and help them grow as needed.

We need to be willing to ask awkward questions, say hard things, and exercise discernment in our evaluations. Often small character flaws can become big problems. Be willing to ask yourself whether these individuals are faithful. Will they complete a task they are given, or do they need a lot of prodding and hand-holding? Are they trustworthy with money, time, responsibilities, and the truth? Are they people we would trust with significant responsibility in our own church?

The apostle Paul gives us two helpful lists of character qualities for elders in 1 Timothy 3:1–7 and Titus 1:5–9 that should, in some measure, characterize everyone we send as missionaries, whether elders or not. Yes, we want to be

43

realistic and allow room for growth. But unless a missionary team wants to take on someone who needs significant character development, we should have the courage to tell a person, "Not yet." We should never abdicate that role to parachurch organizations.

Assess Fruitfulness

Second, we need to be willing to assess a person's fruitfulness. I realize that gospel fruit comes from God and that a person can be faithful without visible fruit. But this is where evaluation inside a local church can be so helpful.

Let's say I have two couples in my church who want to be sent overseas as missionaries. They both live in the same community and have similar circles of Christian friends. Yet one couple is always having folks into their home and has significant relationships with internationals. And it seems like every other non-Christian who spends time with this family ends up being converted. By contrast, the other couple never seems to build deep relationships with people. They try, but somehow it never works out. They attempt to share the gospel, too, but nobody wants to have a second conversation with them. They initiate discipling relationships, but folks don't really seem to grow. In fact, most of these relationships just die out as folks seek out other opportunities for discipling. Both couples may love God. Both may be doing the best they can. But I will strongly encourage my church to spend money sending the first couple overseas, not the second. A trail of conspicuous fruitfulness in other's lives is one of the grand marks of a good

44

prospective missionary. And, generally, it's a church that can best observe this kind of trail over time.

Assess Bible Knowledge

Third, along with seeing fruitfulness and character, we want to send people who stand out in their knowledge and understanding of the Bible. We can debate how much formal theological *training* missionaries should have. But how much theological *understanding* should they have? Everyone who wants to see the gospel accurately transmitted and sound churches established should care about the latter. Take a cue from 1 Timothy 4:16 or Titus 1:9. Doctrinal instruction is essential. The reasons for this are (I hope) fairly obvious. Transmitting the gospel takes care and thought. We always want to make sure we are faithfully explaining and summarizing truth from the Bible. But communicating the gospel in a new culture we barely understand, in a language we are still mastering—*that* takes even more thoughtfulness and theological care. Planting biblical churches cross-culturally requires a deep, clear-headed, and biblical understanding of what a church is and does.

If you carefully read Acts and the Epistles, you will notice that heresy, confusion, and syncretism most often occur at the edge of gospel expansion. Therefore, that is where we need our best-equipped people. Such work is not for every Christian who simply loves to share his or her faith. We need to make sure those we send possess deep theological knowledge so that what they teach can be reproduced in the lives of their hearers with accuracy until Christ returns.

EQUIPPING WOULD-BE MISSIONARIES

The role of the local church is not merely to assess but also to actively equip missionaries. We may not know a lot about specific cultures, learning languages, or even historical issues that shape a people's attitudes toward the gospel. But the local church is the perfect place—God's appointed place—to grow Christian character, encourage general fruitfulness, and transmit sound Bible doctrine. We shouldn't let a few things we might not know keep us from faithfully and assertively stewarding the responsibility for missions God has given churches. Churches are where faithful missionaries are made. If our churches do a good job in our basic responsibilities, then we have all we need to raise up godly missionaries.

Meaningful Membership

In my role as a pastor I regularly have members talk to me about a desire for missionary work. They drop by my office looking for help in thinking through their own suitability for missions. They also want advice on preparation and training. Generally they seem to expect a list of books on missions, special international experiences, and specific instruction on cross-cultural gospel work. What I actually tell them is almost always a disappointment. I lean in, as if I'm going to tell them something extraordinary, and say, "Try to be an especially faithful and fruitful member of this local church." Then I lean back, to let them digest the full profundity of my wisdom.

After a minute, I explain further. Yes, there are a few areas unique to missions that we might discuss, but not many. Most importantly I tell them to work at being church members who open up their homes and lives to other people. To get to know people who are different from them in age, ethnicity, or background. To find, and not just respond to, gospel opportunities. To join neighborhood clubs. To come up with a plan to get to know neighbors. To pray regularly for a list of people with whom they hope to share the gospel during the next month, and then do it!

I tell them to be disciplers. Take initiative to reach out to people and deliberately start relationships where the main goal is to help another person grow as a Christian. Look for opportunities to teach the Bible one-to-one or in a small group Bible study. Work to grow in knowledge and skill at explaining biblical truth. Do all this to build the spiritual muscles that God may well use cross-culturally someday.

The core of missions preparation is not missions studies. It is godliness and Bible knowledge and evangelistic zeal and love for Christ's church and a passion to see Christ glorified.

Specific Training

All that is not to say there aren't some special things you can do to help folks prepare for possible missionary service. In my own church we have the creatively named "Missions Reading Group." We read one book a month, write a one-page reflection paper, then discuss the readings for a couple of hours.

When members join, though, they are sometimes surprised at our reading list. We don't start with books about missions. We start by reading about the authority of God's Word. Then we read books about the gospel, evangelism, and the church. We discuss why a clear understanding of all those topics is crucial to faithful missionary work. Only around the sixth month of our ten-month course do we start reading books specifically about the practice of missions. We want to drive home the point that our understanding of the gospel and the church is more important than any specific missionary strategies we might employ. Both are important. But the former content is essential for a missionary.

International Experiences

You should also look for ways to encourage your members, if possible, to travel overseas to participate in gospel work, particularly with other leaders of your congregation. This is wise, though not essential.

I knew a woman in her seventies who moved from her Texas home to be a missionary in the former Soviet Union. She did fine despite it being not only her first international trip but also her first time outside Texas. Extensive travel and international experience are not prerequisites to missionary work. A love for the gospel, a faithful life, an affirming church, and a willingness to go are. Missionaries aren't world travelers with full passports. The best missionaries tend to go to one place and stay there, sometimes for the rest of their lives.

But in our modern world it's often relatively cheap and easy for folks to visit a place before relocating there. And how helpful for a church leader to go with them. They can talk about the experience and see how they do in a new culture. Do they retreat into social media or behind the soundproof wall of iPod earbuds? Or do they embrace the place and the people? Are they making new friends and opening up their lives as best they can? Given the huge investment it takes to place a missionary overseas, spending some money up front on an exploratory trip is probably wise.

Local Engagement with Internationals

Of course, some people don't need to get on an airplane to engage cross-culturally. In many places, large communities of people from restrictive nations can be freely evangelized right where we live. Not only does the presence of internationals in our home cities present good evangelistic opportunities; it also offers a good way to test someone's desire to work full-time across cultures for the gospel. Cross-cultural relationships can make one person feel excited and invigorated, and another exhausted. People who enjoy building relationships with internationals are likely better suited for missionary work. But how will they know unless they experience these kinds of relationships?

PROVIDING GENEROUS FINANCIAL SUPPORT

Not only should our churches send missionaries wisely, but we should support them appropriately. And our support for workers should be as ample as God's Word enjoins. As we commit to send or support missionaries, we should expect our giving to be serious, significant, and sacrificial. Whether we give directly to missionaries or through some cooperative sending agency, our goal should be workers amply supplied so that they lack nothing.

Strangely, Christians sometimes have pietistic notions of

"faith ministry" that push against the Bible at this point. For almost a decade I served on the board of trustees for a large mission sending agency. We were not a perfect organization, and some things were worth critiquing. But over those ten years one frequent criticism from other believers was that we paid our missionaries too much money. Now, I hope I'm generally good at receiving critiques, but I confess that in those cases I tended to just tilt my head quizzically. As we noted earlier, God instructs us to ensure that his missionaries "lack nothing" and are supported in a manner worthy of his own infinite wealth and worth. One could overdo compensation, I suppose, but on average our organization's workers made less than a similar-sized family living in the United States. That hardly seems to exceed the letter or spirit of God's Word. I suspect our support only seemed excessive when compared to the inadequate support of so many other missionaries.

I don't know how the notion of equating poor missionaries with godly missionaries got started. Regardless, our business is to understand and obey God's Word. And that means amply supplying anyone that our churches send out for the sake of Jesus's name. In God's providence, many gospel emissaries will find themselves in want. The book of Acts and subsequent history are full of such accounts. But such times of testing are God's prerogative. For our part, we should labor to be faithful in our task of sending and supporting.

PARTNERING WITH A GOOD SENDING AGENCY

I've hinted at the place and limitations of mission sending agencies. The potential relationship between a church and a mission sending organization is something each sometimes struggles to get right. Who should bear ultimate responsibility for the welfare of missionaries?

Consider an analogy. Some people choose to homeschool their kids. Others entrust their kids to a school. In the first case, the parent is responsible for all the educational decisions—curriculum, schedule, and so forth. In the latter case, the parent delegates many of these decisions to teachers. Both can be fine choices if carefully considered. But in either case, the parents always remain the parents and the child remains their child. Parents are still finally responsible before God.

Sending out church members as missionaries is similar. A few churches may send their own members directly, taking care of everything. Occasionally our church does this (though it is a lot more work than you may think). Most churches, however, use a sending agency to help them send members. Our church normally partners with one. This latter route involves delegating a lot of on-the-ground decision making to that organization. But by either means of sending, the local church still retains a responsibility for the welfare of its missionary. A healthy relationship with a good sending agency can be one of the best places to start in missions. Sadly, however, many churches use parachurch sending organizations in a manner that looks more like abdication than delegation. Praying and sending money is not the only responsibility churches have for the people they send overseas. Conversely, some sending organizations are only too happy to take up responsibilities that Christ gave to the local church.

Still, the centrality of the local church in missions shouldn't

51

imply that there is virtue in churches not cooperating or need-lessly going it alone. As we noted from 3 John and Philippians, Scripture commends cooperation among churches in sending and supporting missionaries. One way this has been done is through organizations that come alongside churches to coop-erate in sending out missionaries. Some organizations serve a defined fellowship of churches, like the International Mis-sion Board of the Southern Baptist Convention, which my own church cooperates with extensively. Others are more general in nature. But the best of these have common characteristics. They offer solid training for new missionaries on topics the local church may be less equipped to handle, like language learning, special cultural concerns, dealing with taxes overseas, com-puter security, or missionary health. Missions agencies can also give the day-to-day supervision and strategic field support that most churches simply cannot provide.

While a sending agency can't transform an immature be-liever into a fruitful missionary with a few weeks or months of training, it still may have much to teach our missionaries. The best agencies refuse to intrude and act like the church, and instead encourage and help, sometimes even impressing upon local churches their important role of caring for the workers they send. Cooperating with a church, agencies can help send workers to difficult locations that most churches would not be able to reach alone.

MAINTAINING LOCAL CHURCH RESPONSIBILITY

For most churches, a good sending agency is a valuable part-ner. But whether sending missionaries directly or through an agency, the local church should retain responsibility for the welfare of those sent. What does it look like for a local church to care well for its missionaries? At its core, it means working deliberately to know their needs and act for their good. Here are just a few important areas to consider.

Regular Communication

The foundation of a congregation's ability to care for its missionaries is regular communication. We can't meet needs we don't know about, and it's hard to meet pastoral needs if relationships atrophy. Thankfully, it's probably never been easier to keep up relationships from afar. With email and Skype, there is generally no reason to fall out of touch with workers. But it still takes effort. Busyness, time-zone differences, and sometimes security concerns can push these calls off the agenda. Church leaders should consider setting a regular monthly time when they will call each supported worker. In addition, they might find another member of the church who is willing to keep in regular contact with each missionary and occasionally report back to the congregation.

Pastoral Visits

Along with regular calls or emails, it's hard to overstate the value of occasional pastoral visits to overseas workers. I'm not talking about short-term trips or coming to do projects. I mean a pastor (or elder) visiting missionaries with the sole purpose of seeing how they are doing and encouraging them spiritually. I've seen the power of such visits firsthand.

Once, another elder from our church and I visited a family

working in Central Asia. They had been recently expelled from another country where they had worked for years. They were discouraged. So we arranged to stop in their new city for a few days. They were still settling into a new apartment. Their kids were understandably a mess. Most mealtimes were punctuated by child meltdowns. We couldn't fix their circumstances. We just talked and prayed with them in the evenings, read a few Bible passages aloud, and took a couple of long walks to listen. Within seventy-two hours we were gone. It frankly didn't seem like much. But, as a wise pastor once noted, we are not always the best judges of the fruit of our ministry.

A couple of years later this missionary family was visiting the United States, and the husband came to one of our church's elders' meetings. He told our board of elders about how hard the past few years had been: expulsion and relocation, roadblocks and resistance. Then he recounted how he and his wife had decided they were done with missions and were discussing heading back to the United States. That was when my fellow elder and I dropped in for that visit. To my astonishment, he said God used our short time with them to remind them of the reason for their sacrifice and to restore their passion to make the gospel known, whatever the cost. The other elder and I looked at each other with disbelief. God in his kindness had used our small effort to accomplish more than we would have imagined.

But it gets even better. Several years after that elders' meeting the missionary family got back into the country from which they'd been expelled. In part because of their continuing efforts, there is now a team of nearly two dozen other missionaries reaching all through that country.

One of the most interesting passages in Acts is where Paul, the pioneer missionary par excellence, turns to his friend Barnabas and says, "Let us return and visit the brothers in every city where we proclaimed the word of the Lord, and see how they are" (Acts 15:36). Paul saw the importance of relationships and the value of checking up on how workers and new churches were doing.

In a similar way, churches who send and support missionaries should be willing to invest valuable time and resources simply to "see how they are." Visits to love them, listen to them, and encourage them through the Bible and prayer may accomplish more than you would imagine. Missionaries need pastoral encouragement and reminders from God's Word. When we value them enough to invest our time in order to do just that, the impact may echo through countless years and innumerable lives.

Sending Short-Term Help

Supporting workers well also means being sensitive about how, when, and whether to send short-term teams to work with them. I'll take up the topic of short-term teams in chapter 6. But for now it's worth noting that not all short-term teams are a help. Sending people at the wrong time or with the wrong skills, or just sending the wrong kind of people, will not help your long-term workers. The best way to make sure short-term work is genuinely helpful is to send teams that your overseas workers request. Make it clear to your long-term missionaries that receiving short-term teams is not a condition of your support. Rather, give them the freedom to direct who should come, when they should come, and even if they should come or not. Anything else is likely to lead to short-term projects that serve your own ends, but at the considerable expense to the workers you claim to want to help.

Extending Hospitality

One of the best ways to care for missionaries is literally to do what the Bible says to do: show hospitality to them (3 John 8). I wish biblical application were always this straightforward. Hospitality is important during brief visits, but even more important during the months-long returns most missionaries make from time to time. During those longer visits home, consider what your church can do to offer free housing to the workers you support. Plan and budget ahead for this. And don't stop with housing. Look for ways to help them be a meaningful part of the congregation. We want our workers to be able to rest, be refreshed, and reconnect with friends and church leaders. They won't be able to do this if financial concerns force them to live far away with relatives or with another church more willing to provide the housing they need.

Providing Additional Teammates

Finally, perhaps the best gift we can give to supported workers is to send them more workers. Most missionaries I know are deeply grateful for our financial support. When done sensitively, they may appreciate our short-term visits. They are grateful when we host them during their visits back home. But more than anything else, what most missionaries long for is more qualified, like-minded brothers and sisters to join them in their labor.

One of the ways to send more workers is to regularly encourage the congregation to pray for God to send some from their number to join specific missionaries, particularly as we pray for those missionaries. We can also encourage members who are thinking about missions to consider first joining workers we already support. If you trust missionaries enough to support them, you should trust them enough to let them recruit from your congregation. When church planting is the goal, missionary teams especially need to be composed of like-minded individuals. The addition of fellow workers from the sending church (or from another church loved and known well) may be one of the best ways to accomplish this like-mindedness.

CONCLUDING THOUGHTS

As long as your church provides for the material needs of missionaries, those missionaries are in some ways accountable to your church, and you are responsible for them. That's the essence of the partnership in the truth that John writes about in 3 John 7. The same idea is stated negatively in 2 John 10, where John tells us to avoid those who teach falsehood and "not receive [them] into your house or give [them] any greeting." We want to consider carefully whom to send. We want to prepare them well through fruitful and faithful work. And we want to send, support, and love them once they are far away. It's a joy and privilege to partner in work like this. It's what a healthy church does. May both those sent and those who send embrace these relationships for one another's good, for the joy of the nations, and for God's greater glory.

4

GETTING THE HOUSE IN ORDER

I loved my first year at college, but it almost killed me. I was an eager student, to say the least. I took twenty-one course credit hours in one semester (a normal full-time load was fifteen) and joined more clubs than I can remember. I was in political clubs, Christian clubs, clubs related to my major, and social clubs. I didn't say no to any good thing. At the end of the semester, while my grades were fine, my health was not. I'd barely slept and I'd lost weight. When I got home that summer my mother took one look at me, asked a few probing questions, and then wisely declared she wouldn't write another check for college unless I reduced my class load by a third and quit half my clubs.

She was right. What looked like zeal was really youthful foolishness, with a measure of pride thrown in. It was a hard lesson to learn that I'm a finite, limited being.

There's a good chance your church needs to learn the same lesson about global missions. Too many churches view the breadth of their missions commitments, rather than the depth, as the measure of their love for the nations. I've seen many a church hall adorned with a map sprouting pins for every place where the church supports a missionary. That may be just fine, but not if the church assumes that having more pins equals more impact for missions. In reality, it often means the opposite—meager support to a bunch of missionaries barely known by the congregation. But what if we turned breadth and depth on their heads? What if a church gave the same amount of money, but instead of fifty pins there were only five or ten? Or lots of pins in a large church, but in only three or four places around the world. How might that change things?

Even a modest-sized congregation could likely give significant financial support to a few workers. And think about the relationships. With supported workers in only a few places, the possibility exists for substantial financial support, regular communication, pastoral visits, and hosting them when they return home for furlough. It would also allow your congregation to actually learn about the limited places where you are engaged. Members wouldn't be confounded by an overwhelming array of superficial relationships. Instead, they could focus themselves on one or two and really get to know their missionaries and the places they serve.

Similarly, I've known churches whose missions commitments seemingly encompassed every good activity imaginable. From orphanages to education, from radio broadcasts to student evangelism, they committed to every good thing that came their way. Make no mistake, all of those can be good things. But at some point we have to say no, even to good things. We have to prioritize, focus, and decide what's most important for our church.

I know about the value and difficulty of this kind of focus firsthand. In my own congregation I had the dubious distinction of being the "missionary hatchet man" some years ago. I helped lead us in paring down our roster of missionary support from dozens we barely knew to a handful we hoped to invest in deeply. That sounds good in theory, but until you have made a sweet sister in Christ cry as you explain why you are eliminating her support, you may not grasp why this was so hard. That's probably why so many churches collect missionaries but never evaluate and remove them for anything other than gross moral failure.

Now, before some think us cruel, we went about this with great care. We contacted all our supported workers and surveyed their work. We talked together as leaders about whom we would keep and whom we would eliminate from support, and then we gave our workers three years' lead time. We notified them of our intent the first year, kept full support in the second year, reduced it to half-support in the third, and fully eliminated it only at the beginning of the fourth. Even doing that was emotionally wrenching for many. But it needed to be done. We simply couldn't focus on so many places and projects and do it well.

How did we decide whom to keep or to let go? Many were doing good things. But as we looked through the lens of the Bible, three principles stood out. First, we focused on work that aimed to plant and/or strengthen local churches. Second, we focused on work being done well theologically and methodologically. Third, we focused on work and workers with whom we could have significant relationships. Let's consider each one of these three ideas in turn.

FOCUS ON THE LOCAL CHURCH

Usually, the most strategic work we can support is work that aims to establish healthy local churches. This can mean two things. It may mean pioneer evangelism and church planting among a group of people largely unreached by the gospel. Or it may mean laboring to strengthen local churches in places where they exist but are weak, poorly taught, and vulnerable. We find examples of both presented as strategic missionary work in the pages of the Bible.

Pioneer church planting was the heartbeat of the apostle Paul. That was his passion when he penned the words of Romans 15:20–21:

Thus I make it my ambition to preach the gospel, not where Christ has already been named, lest I build on someone else's foundation, but as it is written,

"Those who have never been told of him will see,
and those who have never heard will understand."

Such work remains critically strategic today. While statistics vary widely, most agree that only a tiny portion (maybe 20 percent or less) of Protestant missionaries labor in the least-reached half of the world's peoples. The remaining 80 percent or more work among peoples with significant gospel access and established Christian churches.

What this means for your own missionary support seems clear. Suppose you have funds to support only one worker and must choose between two, both competently engaged in evangelism and church planting. One is working among a people with hundreds of churches and thousands of Christians. The other is laboring in a highly restricted nation with only a few Christians and hardly any churches. All other things being equal, you should generally fund the work among the unreached. I know there are extenuating circumstances, and strategies to reach the unreached from a more reached place exist. Yet the general leaning of the New Testament seems to be toward churches spreading the gospel to "those who have never been told of him."

That work of evangelism should aim to establish local churches. That's what we see throughout the Bible. Granted, there is no Bible verse that says, "Go and plant churches." But we know that all Christians should gather into local churches, "not neglecting to meet together" (Heb. 10:25). And everywhere the missionaries in the book of Acts saw a harvest of souls, a church was soon gathered (Acts 14:1–23; 18:8; 19; 20). The goal of missions is to gather churches that plant other churches.

But pioneer work isn't the only missionary work we see commended in Scripture as strategic. In the beginning of the letter to Titus, we read these words from the apostle Paul: "This is why I left you in Crete, so that you might put what remained into order, and appoint elders in every town as I directed you" (Titus 1:5). Putting churches into better biblical order also was high on Paul's agenda, and it should probably be higher on our agenda too. It can be exciting to send and support workers who are pushing back the boundary of darkness in a community unreached by the gospel. But Paul also demonstrates that it is worth investing some of our best people in church strengthening where the gospel is already known and churches already exist. In a similar way, Paul reminds his young co-missionary Timothy:

> As I urged you when I was going to Macedonia, remain at Ephesus so that you may charge certain persons not to teach any different doctrine, nor to devote themselves to myths and endless genealogies, which promote speculations rather than the stewardship from God that is by faith. (1 Tim. 1:3–4)

Along with helping churches to be biblically structured, Paul wants to establish sound, robust biblical doctrine and to guard new churches against error and false teaching. He is willing to invest perhaps his most valued associate not in his pioneering work in Macedonia but in the ongoing work of building healthy churches in Ephesus. Perhaps we who love new vistas and greater speed should more readily heed Scripture's instruction in this regard.

Many of us can imagine what pioneer mission work looks like, but strengthening ongoing church work may be harder to picture. It doesn't mean encouraging missionaries to hold on to the reins of leadership in a church long after capable local leaders have emerged. That has been done, and the fruit is generally quite poor. Rather, it means purposefully empowering and equipping leaders for emerging local churches. It may mean working for church health in communities where the churches have been long established but are neglected and weak. In a more formal and traditional sense, it may mean teaching in a Bible college or training local church planters in an established local church. More informally, it may mean discipling and training church leaders in a worker's home in a more restricted-access country. The point is that once churches are organized, there will often still be strategic work to do by outside missionaries. We shouldn't let our good passion to find lost sheep in new pastures fool us into neglecting flocks that have already been gathered, purchased by Christ's precious blood.

FOCUS ON WORK THAT'S BEING DONE WELL

We should also focus our support on workers who are excellent in both their theology and their personal practice. Often churches and individuals seem hesitant to evaluate too deeply the theology and quality of the workers they might support. This seems entirely wrongheaded to me. If a worker is offended that you want to explore the contours of his or her theology, that should be a huge red flag. Most workers I've known over the years have been only too happy to discuss their personal theology. Initially, you might ask them to affirm the theological statement affirmed by your church. Use judgment to determine how much variance from your own church's beliefs is okay. Asking what books have influenced them in ministry is another way to explore their theology. Of course, visiting and getting to know missionaries at a personal level is the best way to find out what they believe.

Specifically, you want to probe a missionary or missionary

candidate on two things—the gospel and the church. I've met missionaries who, I trust, love the gospel but couldn't clearly articulate it to save their life, or didn't seem to grasp the importance of concepts like repentance or the Trinitarian nature of the gospel. More often, I've encountered persons sent out with the title of church planter who were stymied when asked, "What is a church and what does it do?" Some just didn't know; others gave answers steeped in personal preference and devoid of Bible. But a few, with the loving tone of a man describing his wife, launched into a Bible-saturated description of the essential marks of a church and its biblical function. Support those missionaries!

Similarly, you want to evaluate the quality of missionaries' personal practice, both in their ministry and in any other work they are doing in their field of service. Ask probing questions. If a missionary is offended that you ask for a description of what she did during the past week or month, be concerned. Many missionaries work in contexts with little direct supervision. Most are faithful, but as fallen human beings, some will not be. A willingness to move overseas for the gospel doesn't say anything about their character, competence, or work ethic. Do they have a good reputation with other expats and locals, as best you can determine?

This concern should extend to any secular pursuits they may be involved in, too. If a missionary runs a business as a means to having a visa in a nation hostile to the gospel, ask about that business. Is he really doing the things he claims to be doing, or is he actively lying to his host government? The cause of the gospel is seldom served by missionaries who lie about their work in order to gain access for the truth. This is an area with some shades of grey, but in general we should hold our workers accountable to integrity and truthfulness in all things. How do we hold them accountable? At the most basic level, we do that by giving money to those who seem to be working with integrity, and withholding support from those who are not.

However, as you vet workers, keep in mind the balance of their time and your level of financial support. This may sound carnal, but you can't give a missionary a few hundred dollars a year and expect him or her to spend a lot of time answering your personal inquiries. This brings us back to my earlier advice about focusing your support on a few relationships. If your congregation gives a significant portion of a missionary's financial needs, that changes things, doesn't it? Then it's reasonable to expect the missionary to reciprocate the commitment your church has demonstrated by financial support. Since we all have limited money to pass around, we want to support missionaries who work with excellence in all things.

FOCUS ON PEOPLE YOU KNOW AND TRUST

We also want the missionaries we support to be known not only by church leaders but by the broader congregation. It is too easy for pastors or missions leaders to get excited about supporting a missionary they've known from college or met at a conference. That can be a good starting point. But if we want our missions support to be congregational, then it needs to involve not just our church's money but also our relationships.

Probably the best way to do this is through extending

hospitality to your missionaries, particularly during their extended return visits to your country. This can be expensive, but the fruit in relationships is priceless. Your relationships will also grow stronger as you find ways to send members, and especially church leaders, to spend time with your workers overseas. Relationships are critical.

Beware of a Focus on Speed, Numbers, and Magic Bullets

A word of caution needs to be said as we consider our missions engagements. As we evaluate missions projects, agencies, and workers we need to realize that our natural affinity for speed, big numbers, and shortcuts can sometimes lead to tragic results in missions.

I've personally visited several countries where well-meaning missionaries became so urgent in their desire for speed and numbers, and so careless in their methods, that new churches were declared planted and then abandoned in a manner resembling spiritual abortions more than births. Their desire for shortcuts meant that the slow work of patient biblical teaching was cast aside. Predictably, these new gatherings easily fell prey to false teaching, cults, or simply dissolution. A decade later the wounds have yet to heal. Most tragically, countless souls in these places now think they've seen and tried Christianity, when they haven't. As a result, they are seemingly inoculated against the real, biblical gospel, even if someone more faithful shares it with them. God forgive us.

The work of missions is urgent, but it's not frantic. We long for a harvest, but God has nowhere guaranteed a rate of increase. Instead, when we look to the Bible, we see a repeated concern that God's missionaries would never abandon patient, diligent faithfulness. Perhaps this is nowhere more striking than in Paul's charge to his fellow missionary church planter in arms, Timothy. Paul declares:

> In the presence of God and of Christ Jesus, who will judge the living and the dead, and in view of his appearing and his kingdom, I give you this charge: Preach the word; be prepared in season and out of season; correct, rebuke and encourage—with great patience and careful instruction. (2 Tim. 4:1–2 NIV)

Those final words—"with great patience and careful instruction"—should ring in our ears as we evaluate our missionary efforts and partnerships. God knows we may be tempted by a desire for immediate, visible results, leading to missionaries who are impatient and careless, slapdash and superficial.

What might have happened if churches over the last century had been wise enough to withhold support from work that seemed too good to be true, or had dared to ask more probing questions about the numbers reported? What might have happened if they had been relationally engaged and had gently guided errant work back onto the path of urgently patient faithfulness? We can't change the past, but with God's help we can do better going forward.

Careless methods for church planting aren't our only danger. Our natural affinity for speed, volume, and ease can also lead us to bypass existing churches. Especially if their numerical impact has been slight, we may be tempted to ignore indigenous churches as defective or, even more tellingly, irrelevant. Still, what might the impact be if, instead of ignoring them, we engaged them, both to learn from them and help them? Even if they lack some beloved modern methods for multiplication, isn't it possible they might know something about the culture that we don't?

When we learn the value of existing churches, the impact can be deep, lasting, and glorious. I know a missionary in a large eastern European city with several million Muslim guest workers from all across Central Asia. He moved there to try to reach, train, and mobilize Muslim converts. He encouraged them to return to their home nations to plant disciple-making churches throughout Central Asia. Yet, unlike many missionaries, he didn't ignore the local Protestant churches in his city, even though they had a reputation for suspicion and disdain toward their Muslim neighbors. While he personally worked to reach Muslim immigrants with the gospel, he also invested in existing churches from the majority culture. He built trust. He looked for local Christians with gospel maturity. Then, slowly, he began to connect them with Muslim converts. They were amazed to meet former Muslims who had genuinely embraced the truth of Christ and were passionate to return home with that message. Then, building on years of experience evangelizing Muslims, he began to help local church leaders develop efforts to evangelize Muslims themselves.

On a recent visit with this friend, I sat in the small parlor of his Soviet-era apartment. As I drank tea and looked out at the masses milling about in the park below, I asked about prospects for the future. The situation for foreigners was getting more complicated. The possibility of being forced out by the government was looming larger. My friend and his wife were grieved at the idea that they might have to leave the city and people they loved. But then he looked across his tea and told me, with a kind of unflinching confidence, that it was too late. Even if the government deported them right then, their ministry and passion for reaching Muslim immigrants had spread across half a dozen local churches and was spreading farther and faster all the time. Just a few months earlier, some of those churches had, on their own, hosted a meeting to encourage and train other churches in Muslim evangelism. The torch had been set to the wood. Banishing the torchbearer now would accomplish nothing.

I found myself pondering how things might have been different if this couple had decided to go it alone. What if they had believed their Western methodologies were superior to the existing local churches and so ignored them entirely? What if they had been so committed to rapidly planting new churches that they felt they had no use for the churches doing gospel work for generations in that culture? Thankfully, they didn't make these mistakes. As a result, I expect their impact will quietly continue among these other churches until Christ returns.

Partner with Those Who Pursue Faithfulness

What does this mean as we consider whom to support? It means that we should prioritize efforts that center on the local church, either through church planting or church strengthening. While there are certainly other good works we may support as individuals and churches, those two categories seem to be the norm from Scripture and the focus of missions for most of the past two thousand years. Both are worth investing our best people in, just as the apostle Paul did.

Again, this likely means asking occasionally awkward questions of missionaries and organizations. Ask what their plan is to see local churches planted. Some groups have a vision to see a whole movement established, where hundreds of churches plant thousands of churches in a kind of fast-motion chain reaction. This might be a wonderful thing for which to hope and pray. But ask these groups how they intend to see the first churches planted and how they hope to train leaders and establish sound doctrine. The answers to those questions are far more important than the grand scope of their vision. Likewise, others may talk more about new foolproof methods than about the Bible. New methods are fine (if they square with the Bible), but if any worker or organization sells them as a new "key" to unlocking the nations for Christ, hold on to your wallet and run away.

Whether great things happen in our time or not is in God's control. We are all called to be faithful in both fruitful and lean times. Success is in the hands of God. This means that we should support missionaries and organizations that understand the biblical commands for urgently faithful perseverance; don't be distracted by grand promises of quick, easy shortcuts. Get-rich-quick schemes are always attractive but are rarely a substitute for hard work and faithfulness.

It's not only for our sake that we should be careful, but also for the sake of the souls of the missionaries we support. As the old British pastor Charles Bridges noted, "The seed may lie under the clods until we lie there, and then spring up."[1] In other words, good gospel work won't always yield immediate visible results. Sometimes we may not live to see the harvest. This is a hard reality for anyone to accept. Missionaries are no different. Many have been tempted to disregard biblical teaching or even to modify the gospel message itself to produce the appearance of results when real success is slow.

But we, as their supporters, should be a help, not a hindrance, in this regard. We should never take up Satan's work by tempting them to sin through pressuring them toward unfaithfulness. Yet we do that when we demand metrics with an implied link to their support. If we subtly communicate a desire for a certain quota of baptisms, as some have done, we may unwittingly be taking up Peter's role from Matthew 16:23. There our Lord rebukes him, saying, "Get behind me, Satan! You are a hindrance to me. For you are not setting your mind on the things of God, but on the things of man." Let the Devil do his own work. We needn't help him.

5

HEALTHY MISSIONS PARTNERSHIPS

Ask several missionaries about partnerships with churches, and you might hear radically different stories.[1] Some will tell about overbearing churches that thought they had all the answers and never stopped to ask questions or learn, or about endless emails and Skype calls in an effort to get on the same page, only to end in frustration. Other missionaries will glow when telling you about churches that got to know them, respected them, and seemed only to want to serve them. Listen closely to a missionary talking about a good relationship with a supporting church, and I bet you will be able to smell the aroma of humility, with a generous accent of trust.

TRUST AND HUMILITY—TWO SIDES OF A COIN

Trust and humility go together. Where there is trust, it is easier to act in humility. And humility will generally show itself in trust. Trust is the soil in which humility grows best. But building good relationships may not look like an especially humble undertaking at the outset.

The best way to build partnerships marked by humility is to be ruthlessly selective about whom you will partner with. In a partnership without a reasonable level of trust, one party cannot responsibly defer to the other. You can't submit humbly because, without trust, voluntary submission is simply irresponsible. If you believe that a missionary is doing a poor job or conducting himself unwisely, why would you entrust him with funds and people he'd only misuse or mistreat?

Put simply, as you consider establishing a long-term partnership with a missionary, whether one you send or one you adopt, among the first questions you should ask is "Do I really trust this person?" Does he hold to theology about the gospel and the nature and work of the church that you can wholeheartedly support? Does he demonstrate and have a reputation for good judgment and integrity? If he lived in your town, would you want him to be a leader or an elder in your church?

Some people are uncomfortable asking questions of this sort. It can seem narrow or prideful to evaluate a missionary so rigorously. But the alternative is much worse: a relationship marked by second guessing, argument, and working at cross-purposes. Nobody needs that.

SIX CHARACTERISTICS OF A HEALTHY PARTNERSHIP

I want to offer six principles for partnering with overseas workers in global evangelism. Before we get there, let me clarify what these principles are and what they are not. These are not things directly commanded by Scripture. But neither are they mere observations or best practices about what seems to make partnerships work. Instead, these ideas flow from biblical priorities for churches and church planting. Those general priorities include the importance of humility (Phil. 2:1–11; 1 Pet. 5:5), the creating and shaping of God's people by his Word (Ezek. 37:1–14; Matt. 4:4; 2 Tim. 4:1–3), the beauty of cooperation among churches in gospel work (3 John), and the gospel "rightness" of committed love for specific missionaries (Phil. 4:10–20). It's my hope that reflecting on these broad priorities will help churches more carefully consider how they can engage humbly with global gospel work.

1. Servant-Minded

Every partnership begins with the motivations you bring to the table. Are you seeking to serve workers overseas or to be served by them? Don't just pass this by with a mental wave of the hand—think about it honestly. Many churches seem to view missions partnerships as a way to enhance their own "missions program" rather than as an avenue to serve Christ by serving his missionaries.

Bolstering your own image is a really strange thing for Christians to do. From the Bible it is clear that God's redeemed people should always be marked by humility. How ironic to labor in another culture to bring glory to Christ while approaching it with selfishness or pride. Instead, we should strive for humility in our international partnerships because we desperately need grace. In this as in all things, "God opposes the proud but gives grace to the humble" (1 Pet. 5:5).

A servant-minded posture is especially important for churches that have enjoyed a measure of numerical success at home. It's easy for even a right sense of thankfulness and confidence to translate into a prideful assumption that you know what's best in another culture. I've observed absurd conversations where a church leader who knows almost nothing of the language or customs of another culture tried to "take charge" in order to "help" an overseas worker "do evangelism better" and "grow the church." Too often this advice has been based on pragmatic, consumer-driven ideas that are unbiblical and man-centered in any culture. But even when the advice was genuinely wise and biblical, pushing it on a missionary carelessly or too quickly made it unattractive.

Either way, it's better for your church to find people on the field whose judgment and theology you already trust, and then submit to them. When making partnerships (especially those focused on church planting), you should not assume theological agreement but honestly discuss issues like evangelism, ecclesiology, soteriology, and more—*before* entering into a partnership. The fact that both partners call themselves "evangelical" or belong to the same denomination may not be enough.

So what does a humble, servant-minded partnership look like in practice? Well, it's characterized by a desire to do "the ministry of whatever." Being willing to do *whatever* the field workers or missions leaders deem helpful is the right place to begin. It means saying, "What can we do to serve and partner with you? Nothing is too big and nothing is too small."

This willingness to start small and be faithful in an incrementally deepening partnership is hugely important for building trust. Some overseas workers have spent years learning a language and engaging a culture, only to have careless short-term teams from the United States come and blow up years of work. Their fear is legitimate.

But as a church demonstrates a willingness to help foreign workers in even small, behind-the-scenes ways—like caring for children while their parents attend training meetings—it earns the workers' trust as well as the opportunity to gently propose biblically based change.

2. Pastor-Led

Leadership begins not with the pastor's own passion for missions—that's great but insufficient. It begins with a pastor regularly preaching through the whole corpus of Scripture, opening up the implications of the gospel Sunday after Sunday. God is a missionary God. He has a passion for the nations, and Scripture is full of that passion. From the books of Moses, through the histories, to the Prophets, and on throughout the Gospels and Epistles, God's passion to call worshipers from all languages, tribes, people, and nations is foundational (see Gen. 12:2–3; Isa. 19:19–25; or Rev. 7:9–10 for just a taste).

Congregations whose shepherds regularly preach this rich biblical message will begin to have their worldview shaped by it. They will learn that the gospel is about more than merely growing "their" church. It's about more than their own culture or country. The gospel is for all people everywhere. Understanding both the urgency of the task—"How will they hear unless someone is sent?"—and the greatness and worthiness of God will fuel a passion that touches a whole congregation. Preaching like this is in fact the most foundational thing a pastor can do to lead his congregation in missions.

A pastor must not only preach; he must also pray regularly from the pulpit for the work of the gospel overseas. This instructs the hearts of his people as they hear that God's kingdom is about more than just "our group." It exposes their minds to God's vast global plan. Such prayer reminds them each Sunday that Jesus is Lord of the people of Tobago and Uzbekistan and Bhutan as well as their home town.

John Stott, a noted British pastor, once visited a small church in an English village. Upon hearing the content of the pastoral prayer, which never strayed beyond the interests of their small community, he summed them up, saying, "I came away saddened, sensing that this church worshipped a little village god of their own devising. There was no recognition of the needs of the world, and no attempt to embrace the world in prayer."[2] Prayer from the pulpit that embraces the global cause of Christ is one of the best antidotes to such God-belittling provincialism. Such prayer can do more than you may imagine to expand the hearts of a congregation.

Finally, a pastor who faithfully shapes his congregation's passions by the Word can then show them how to direct their passions by going out himself to support the work of missions. He should not go alone but should take key leaders with him. When a pastor demonstrates the importance of cross-cultural gospel work by giving his own time to it, the impact on the congregation can be huge.

Our own congregation's current engagement with partnerships in Central Asia can be traced, in part, to a trip in 2000 when our senior pastor traveled to Turkey to speak at a meeting of missionary workers. This pastoral example helped jump-start a partnership that has now grown to be one of the key missions engagements for our congregation.

3. Relationship-Based

Partnerships shouldn't be based on projects but on personal relationships. Often we're tempted to think that we need to have our fingers in many places around the world in order to be faithful to the Great Commission. But keeping up with many contacts in many places often results in shallow and ineffectual relationships.

As we saw at the outset of chapter 4, in most cases churches would do better to pick a few workers and go deep in their relationship with their work. This kind of focus requires a humble admission that while God is infinite, you and your congregation are not. And it requires the loving discipline to resist overextending your congregation into shallow, feel-good engagements every time you hear about some new opportunity. But the results for the kingdom can be striking when this sort of discipline and focus prevails.

Again, when evaluating whom to invest in, three principles have proven helpful to our church. We try to partner with workers who are the following:

- *Excellent in their work.* We want to partner with workers who seem to be doing work well and who are biblically thoughtful about how they do it.
- *Strategic in their focus.* We want to partner with workers laboring in places where there is little gospel light or where their work aims to strengthen local churches.

- *Widely known by the congregation.* We want to partner with workers who not only are known to the church leadership but are known (or willing to do the work to become known) throughout the whole congregation.

If you partner with workers from outside your congregation, you should think about their level of relationship with your congregation at the outset. This may mean making a trip to visit them on the field before you officially partner with them. Ideally they could spend extended time living among your members. I'm not talking about a long weekend; I'm talking about months. Inviting workers to spend their entire stateside assignment with your congregation and providing them free housing is a great way to do this.

In our church we generally won't officially partner with workers until we have been able to spend extended time with them, forming relationships between them and the congregation. It may slow things down initially, but the long-term fruit in everyone's lives seems worth it.

4. Commitment-Centered

Your church should be willing to seriously commit to the workers with whom you partner. Workers all too often tell of churches who mean well but turn out to be fair-weather partners, or who lose interest in a partnership when situations on the field limit their involvement in short-term trips or projects. Instead, consider committing to serve a team of workers in any way they find helpful. Be willing to do trips if they find that helpful. Be willing *not* to come if the timing isn't right.

Being commitment-centered also means working with a long attention span, for the long haul. In good years and bad. When your partnership is encouraging or just plain hard.

Finally, this commitment should show itself in a desire to celebrate thoughtful biblical faithfulness, even if fruit is slow in coming. By doing this you can help the workers with whom you partner to resist the seductive call of immediate visible results that has caused so many workers to first tweak and then further distort the gospel in pursuit of quick "success." Your commitment to faithfulness can help your partnering workers to persevere in proclaiming the plain gospel message even when the results aren't seen.

5. Congregation-Wide

It also should come as no surprise that a healthy church partnership generally presumes that the congregation, not just a few leaders, actually owns the partnership. When the average church member understands something of the focus and direction of the church's partnership, then the ground is laid for a fruitful relationship. This can be encouraged by regularly updating the entire congregation on the church's international involvement. In my own church this is done through a short report during members meetings and through regular prayers for missionaries on Sunday nights.

To get to this point our congregation has tried to teach that active concern for missions is a normal part of the faithful Christian life, not an optional add-on. For us this has also meant eliminating special mission committees and giving oversight of our missions efforts to the church elders. This has helped members see that missions is a core part of the ministry of the church, not one among many optional ministries on the periphery, for certain people who are "interested in that sort of thing."

It's also important to involve the congregation in praying for missions. In our own congregation, we hear a brief one-to-two-minute update, every Sunday night, for a worker we support (out of about twenty, total) and then pray for him or her. We regularly host workers when they are in town and interview them before the whole congregation. Then we pray for them. We also print the names and general details of our supported workers in a prayer directory given to every member of our church. As much as security concerns allow, we put the names and general locations of our workers in front of all members, not just the "missions club."

6. Long-Term Focused

Finally, most fruitful and humble partnerships will almost certainly be long-term focused. By this I mean that your church should work to cultivate long-term overseas workers from your own congregation. At the outset of a partnership, why not articulate the explicit goal that some of your own members will uproot their lives and plant them long-term in another culture for the sake of the gospel? Even more, if possible, why not aim to eventually staff an entire missionary team from your church or in partnership with other like-minded churches? Having a team that is on the same theological page right from the start won't solve every problem, but it will certainly avoid many.

Being long-term focused may also mean doing short-term

trips with the long-term mind-set. Rather than just providing "missions experiences," consider trips that support the work of existing long-term teams to whom you are committed. See your short-term work primarily as a way to support your long-term partners in whatever ways they need, and secondarily as a way to raise up your own members to join the work long-term. Workers on the mission field generally need more boots on the ground—day in, day out—not just friends passing through.

CONCLUDING THOUGHTS

These six qualities will go a long way toward making your partnerships more God-glorifying and, frankly, more fruitful for everyone. At some point you may need more clarity and more agreement on specific roles and responsibilities. Even as you spell those out, it's best to treat a partnership more like a family adoption or a marriage and less like a contract or corporate merger. There may be a time for written documents, but the place to start missions partnerships is with relationships, humility, and trust.

Godly partnerships are important not only with individual missionaries or indigenous workers but also with parachurch organizations. As best we can, we want to know the people who are directly supervising our members or those with whom we partner. Many of these principles of relationships and trust and commitment apply to them as well.

Treating love and mutual respect as the basis for missions partnerships is not just a prudent idea; it's a biblical one. In Paul's letter to the Philippians we see wonderful glimpses of a healthy long-term missionary partnership based on trust and relationship: "For God is my witness, how I yearn for you all with the affection of Christ Jesus" (Phil. 1:8). It was a bond characterized by long-term commitment: ". . . because of your partnership in the gospel from the first day until now" (Phil. 1:5). Paul's letter drips with love and mutual concern and committed, long-term support. That's a noble aim for us in our missionary partnerships. Like Paul and the Philippians, we also want to look back on years of partnership and say with joy and confidence, "To our God and Father be glory forever and ever. Amen" (Phil. 4:20).

6

REFORMING
SHORT-TERM MISSIONS

In February 1812, Adoniram Judson boarded a ship bound for India, leaving home and hearth for the sake of the gospel. Before his departure he sold most of his possessions and bid a tearful goodbye to his family and friends. He would not return to the United States for more than thirty years, and then only for one short visit. He died in India in 1850, after thirty-seven years of missionary service, mostly in Burma. Judson's experience was fairly typical for missionaries of his generation.

Two centuries later, in February 2012, Tony also headed to India for the sake of the gospel. But unlike Judson, he didn't sell anything (other than some cupcakes at a fundraiser). He didn't bid a tearful goodbye to family and friends. Nor did he stay overseas for thirty years before coming home. In fact, as he boarded the aircraft bound for India, he already had a return ticket for his flight home in two weeks. In this regard Tony, like Judson before him, was also typical of missionaries of his own generation.

The advent of international short-term mission trips has

probably done more than anything else to change the world-wide missions landscape. Our fictional Tony represents that shift. It's estimated that more than a million North Americans participate in short-term mission trips overseas each year, up from an estimated twenty-five thousand in 1980. During this same period, long-term missionaries from North America have only increased slightly, if at all.[1] This trend prevails in other nations too.

What are we to make of this massive shift of resources? Is it a good or bad thing? How can our churches wisely respond to this trend? Most importantly, what does the Bible tell us about short-term missions and God's place for them in his global mission for his church?

PAUL'S SHORT-TERM MISSION TRIPS?

In their excellent book *Mack and Leeann's Guide to Short-Term Missions*,[2] Mack and Leeann Stiles begin by briefly survey-ing examples of short-term missions in the Bible. They trace the route and description of Paul's first missionary journey and note some interesting points. First, Paul was seldom in any city more than a few months. Second, the entire journey took only about a year and a half before he was back home at his sending church in Antioch. One might reasonably argue that Paul's first journey was really just a series of consecutive short-term mission trips. It's a helpful observation for anyone tempted to discount short-term work prematurely.

However, there are also a few qualifications to keep in mind. For one thing, Paul never seems to have needed to learn a new language to communicate the gospel where he traveled.

The ubiquity of Greek throughout the Mediterranean world made that largely unnecessary. And with few exceptions his short-term trips seem to have been unintentionally short—meaning that in almost every case he left because of opposition or rejection, not because of an intentional short-term strategy. How long he might have stayed under different circumstances is unknowable. Still, there are a few times when he seems to have planned to stay in a place only for a short period of time (Acts 20:1–2). But most of those trips were visits to existing gatherings of Christians (Acts 20:5–7), not efforts to establish new churches. No, short-term missions are not unbiblical, but neither are they held up in Scripture as a preferred method for spreading the gospel and planting new churches. And historically they have never been common, until recently.

Without explicit biblical direction on this question, we need to think carefully and rely on wisdom and the overall narrative of Scripture. When we do, a number of concerns about short-term missions (at least as often practiced from North American sending churches) become apparent. To be clear, I am not suggesting that we abandon all short-term trips in light of these concerns. Rather, if we want short-term efforts to be truly helpful, we need to seriously consider these concerns and how to mitigate them.

CONCERNS ABOUT SHORT-TERM TRIPS

One problem with many short-term trips is how we plan and promote them. Not infrequently churches promote short-term trips by talking about the good of getting "missions experience" or the opportunity "to make a difference in the world."

Prior participants tell potential short-termers how a trip positively impacted or even revolutionized their faith. I don't doubt this, but it often seems that our short-term trips can be more about us and our experiences than about encouraging gospel work and glorifying God. Such a misdirection is no small matter. It's often been said that "what we win people *with* is what we win them *to*." If we promote short-term missions based on thinking about our benefits, we run the risk of making short-term missions a selfish enterprise.

Ironically, the cost of this kind of thinking is largely borne by the long-term missionaries we are ostensibly seeking to help. If we go on a trip because of what it may do for us, even if the thing desired is good (like spiritual growth), it is likely we will expect local workers to make sure we get the experience we desire. The end result is that many missionaries dread short-term visits and view hosting them as a necessary evil in order to maintain relationships with churches back home. That is both tragic and needless.

At other times short-term work is disconnected from missionaries or long-term work altogether. This creates its own problems. In such cases short-term work can take on a "drive by" character as teams pass through a town to share their message, perhaps though drama or music, but with no way to evaluate responses to the gospel or to connect interested people to local Christians or churches. Of course, this assumes there is an intent to proclaim the gospel associated with the trip. It seems an increasing number of North American short-term trips don't aim at proclaiming the gospel. Many understand missions as doing good things, perhaps in the name of Christ, but without connecting their ministry to gospel declaration. Or perhaps they serve a local congregation in a way that makes them unhelpfully dependent. All of these are problematic in their own ways.

Added to that, most short-term missionaries don't have the language and cultural skills during their brief stays to ever rival a long-term missionary in effectiveness. In areas more hostile to the gospel, this lack of cultural understanding can mean that short-termers end up saying and doing things that actually hurt the work of missionaries and local Christians. They can set back the true work of the gospel by encouraging uninformed gospel "decisions" among locals.

For instance, a Hindu woman may be happy to raise her hand and pray a prayer to Christ as Savior. Naive short-termers go home reporting her "decision for Jesus," not realizing that she has merely added one more god to the vast collection of deities she worships. But it's worse than that, because if a Christian later tries to accurately explain the gospel, she's more likely to ignore her, thinking, "I've already done Christianity. I pray to Jesus on Tuesdays, and Vishnu on Wednesdays."

Short-term workers can also engage in evangelistic methods that are unnecessarily socially disruptive and actually invite persecution that continues to haunt locals long after the short-termers have safely flown home with their photos and stories.

All of these concerns are compounded by the cost of short-term trips. Given the expense of travel, most short-term workers cost vastly more per week than a similar long-term worker. To fund short-term trips, churches sometimes divert resources from effective long-term work, and this can actually hinder the overall work of the gospel.

So it's often not a pretty picture. At the risk of being excruciatingly blunt: a thoughtful evaluation of short-term mission trips will reveal that many are ineffective, distracting, wasteful, and in some cases flat-out counterproductive to the cause of Christ among the nations.

SHORT-TERM MISSIONS THAT HELP

With all that said, should we just scrap all short-term trips from our churches? No. But many churches may need to give serious thought to reforming them in ways that mitigate these frequent pitfalls. Where that is done, short-term trips can be a significant aid and encouragement to long-term gospel work, as well as a blessing to the individuals who go and the churches that send them.

This necessary change starts before anyone gets on an airplane. It starts with how we think about our goal for a short-term mission trip. Whom do we really intend to benefit most? Here's a big hint—it shouldn't be ourselves or our churches. From the very beginning we should decide that every short-term trip will aim to benefit the work of long-term missionaries and local believers. Most simply, this means building relationships of trust with people in a place where we hope to labor. It also means asking them what, if anything, they want us to do and, whenever possible, doing exactly what they ask.

Again, this is why churches should focus their financial support on missionaries whom they know and who are doing good work aimed at church planting or strengthening. We want to send short-term workers based on the same criteria. Normally this will involve sending most, if not all, our short-term workers to serve people we already support. It might result in our churches taking fewer short-term trips, but the trips taken would much more likely be useful.

Keeping the Long Term in View

Committing to this will mean doing short-term missions with a decidedly long-term view. That means two things, really.

First, you should make sure that your short-term trips are usefully connected to long-term works you know well and support. It also means letting the folks overseas decide when, if, and to what end your members will come. This may produce short-term trips that are less appealing to your church members on the front end, but it will better serve the long-term workers on the back end.

For example, one of the most frequent short-term trips that my church makes is to help host meetings for our long-term missionaries. This includes doing things like watching their children so that they can attend training seminars. Why? Because this is what they tell us they want. Often missionaries need this kind of everyday help, but they cannot hire local unbelievers, lest the unbelievers turn them in to unfriendly governments. And they cannot hire local believers, lest the locals get arrested by unfriendly governments. So my church's members happily travel around the world to take care of children and do other behind-the-scenes work; because, at worst, unfriendly governments will probably just tell us to go home.

But when we humbly reform our short-term work, the

fruit can be profound. I remember a trip to Central Asia where some of our church members from Washington, DC, were caring for missionary kids during a training meeting. It wasn't especially exciting or fun. The meeting place was run down. But one afternoon a missionary couple came to me almost in tears. They had just figured out that the person sitting on the dusty floor playing with their two-year-old and changing diapers all day was a White House official. Say what you want about worldly power and importance. For this missionary couple the idea that someone on a first-name basis with the US president would use vacation time to serve them so humbly was a huge encouragement. Are any of us really too busy or important to serve missionaries like this? Do we honestly care whether our short-term trips are fun or interesting if we can know that they are encouraging and useful?

Second, short-term missions with a long-term view includes an ultimate goal that your short-term work would result in members of your own church someday living long-term in the places to which you have committed. But doing this may also mean that instead of constantly looking for new missions experiences, you should identify just a few strategic places and send people to them over and over, for years.

Occasionally short-term work may also help open up new work in a new place. I know of a few churches that have done this in places where there were no missionaries or local congregations. These churches would identify a strategic area and (usually in partnership with a mission agency) develop a way to send small groups of their members to that place. Often they would visit several times a year to meet people and give out

Bibles, or show an evangelistic film, or just visit as Christian tourists, or even partner in relief work. Through the process they would begin to gain real knowledge about the area and the people. They were plowing the ground, so to speak, and just by their conduct and open identification as Christians they often confounded local hostility to Christ's followers. But what made this work lastingly useful was the aim to send long-term people. Whether it's new work or existing relationships, part of our goal should be to eventually send our own people to join the work long-term.

Preparing for the Short-Term Trip

Once we focus in on church-centered short-term work, how do we prepare participants to serve well? Here are ten points that any participant in a short-term trip should consider.

1. *Be focused on God's glory among the nations.* God is great. He is infinitely worthy to be praised for all the excellences of his nature. In his unfathomable love, God has chosen to glorify himself by showing mercy through Christ to sinful, self-glorifying rebels like you and me. This truth should fill our hearts with wonder and praise (Rom. 15:8–10).

As simple as it may sound, one of the best things you can do to prepare for a trip to support overseas workers is to think deeply about God's greatness and his amazing mercy in the gospel. God deserves to be praised among the nations, and he will in fact be praised and delighted in (see John 10:16; Rev. 5:9). There is nothing like a big view of God's glorious global plan to put our individual concerns and contributions in an appropriately smaller perspective.

2. *Be humble.* We have been redeemed by the One who "humbled himself by becoming obedient to the point of death, even death on a cross" (Phil. 2:8). It would be a tragedy of immense proportion, then, if we should approach our work for him with even a hint of arrogance. Instead we should be humble. We should defer to the field staff, and even to one another, in love. We should be slow to speak. We should not think too highly of ourselves but be quick to serve. Let the aroma of Christ's humility be evident in everything we do and say.

3. *Be prepared to spend yourself and be spent.* Work overseas, with jet lag, and in a strange environment is tiring. Expect to spend yourself to encourage and help your church's workers. And expect to feel like you have been spent. Of course, this may not always be fun, but when you feel tired, think of *why* you are tired. It's the tiredness of extravagantly devoting ourselves to the kingdom of our Lord. Let even your weariness remind you of the worth of the gospel.

4. *Be flexible.* Short-term trips will almost certainly not turn out like you plan. Prepare now to be okay with that. One of the most tangible ways churches can serve overseas workers is by not panicking when plans change and not making demands on the workers to fix everything. Prepare now to happily toss your plans (if needed) and take on the ministry of "whatever." Remind yourself that your ultimate goal is not to execute some task but to encourage men and women who have left much for the sake of the gospel. We will often best encourage them by doing whatever they will find most encouraging, even if it's different from our preferences or plans.

5. *Be a learner.* Part of humility is realizing that you don't know everything and being ready to ask questions and learn. Don't assume that because you know how to do something well at home, you know how to do it well in another context. Honor those who live in the culture by asking questions and being ready to learn from them.

6. *Be encouraging.* Even if we don't know much, there are some things of which we can be absolutely certain. God is good, and he does whatever pleases him (Ps. 115:3; John 10:11). These two truths are the twin pillars of Christian confidence—God is good and God is Lord. Remind missionaries of these two truths in hundreds of different ways. Talk about your own delight in God's kindness and his control. By doing this you will bless missionaries and shore up the foundation of their confidence in their work. If we really understand this reality, what is there to worry about?

7. *Be extravagant in service.* We are told to partner with those who have gone out for the sake of Christ's name by supporting them in a manner worthy of God (3 John 5–8). Be ready to care for your workers extravagantly, even beyond what seems reasonable. Be ready to do that in a manner "worthy of God" himself. This will show not only that we value them as individuals but also that we supremely value the great gospel they carry.

8. *Be low maintenance.* It can be hard to avoid falling into "I'm a tourist—serve me" mode on trips like this. Many workers tell me stories of folks who come to "serve" them only to demand to be entertained, helped, and served. We are often surrounded by amazing places while overseas, and it's totally

97

reasonable to want to enjoy our time so long as it doesn't create an added burden for those we say we have come to serve. Be vigilant about that. Be ready to forgo things you might enjoy in order to serve those you've come to bless. Hopefully you'll find great joy in this, no matter what else you are able to do.

9. *Be patient.* By our patience we show tangible evidence of gospel-saturated humility. When we must ask for something to be done or fixed or explained by mission workers, be patient about their responses. Travel in many countries can be frustrating and inefficient. Many cultures will move at a different pace from our own. And requests that we think are simple can actually take a lot of work on someone else's part. Again, this is one great way we can serve one another and our workers—by being patient and trusting in God, even when things don't move at the pace we prefer.

10. *Be focused on God's glory among the nations.* Of course, all these particulars are just a few applications of the one, central truth with which we began. God is glorious and worthy to be praised. His promise of forgiveness, redemption, and fellowship is worth more than anything else we can have or imagine. The point is not to learn these few simple rules. The point is to look deeply at the gospel and then find ways to apply implications of the gospel to our experience overseas. Saturate yourself with thoughts of the grace given in the gospel, and let that overflow into your words and deeds. If you do that, I'm pretty sure you will be a Christ-glorifying blessing on your trip and in every other aspect of your life.

CONCLUDING THOUGHTS

All this may require adjustments in how some churches think about short-term missions. For others it may require a wholesale overhaul of short-term work. But if this sounds like a biblical approach, if it smells of Christian humility, and if it seems wise, then why wouldn't you make the change?

It may mean disappointing some members who have grown attached to less useful kinds of trips. You will certainly want to be wise and gentle in making changes. But given the amount of money, time, and trouble that go into short-term trips, surely we should think carefully about making them genuinely useful. Isn't that what we ultimately want?

7

ENGAGING THE NATIONS BY OTHER MEANS

The heart of missionary obedience to the Great Commission is sending and supporting gospel workers to gather people into churches across ethnic, cultural, or geographic boundaries (Matt. 18:18–20). That's what we mean by missions. Throughout Christian history, that has been and continues to be the joy and obligation of every faithful church (3 John 7).

But faithfulness to send missionaries this way doesn't preclude any number of other worthy efforts our churches might engage in globally. Some efforts may be implied in other biblical commands. Others are simply ideas to consider. Admittedly, we can't all give attention to everything that might be worthwhile. But here are three other routes to the nations that I hope we don't overlook in our appropriate zeal to send and support missionaries. Some of these may not be missions in the most traditional sense. They don't all have a claim on the resources of the local church. But some church members will have one gift, and others another. After we've done what's clearly commanded, maybe we can still do more. Who knows how many other efforts the Lord might also be pleased to use? And it can start right where we live.

REACHING THE NATIONS AT HOME

Stephen came to the United States from China to study. He was raised as an atheist and thought that if God did exist, he couldn't be personal. God must be distant like the stars or the moon—beyond knowing and beyond our reach.

At his university Stephen began attending free English classes taught by local Christians. He liked the people he met. He appreciated their help with his English, but something more kept him coming. When Michael, one of the English tutors, offered to meet up with him to discuss the Bible, Stephen was happy to do it. For more than a year they met every week. The progress was slow. Language differences were often painful. Some weeks he and Michael were only able to cover one or two verses. But Michael persisted, week after week. Slowly, in fits and starts, Stephen began to understand God and the gospel. More than a year after their first meeting, Michael was present on the Sunday this young former atheist from China was baptized as a Christian.

God has increasingly brought the nations to our doorsteps. That's true for many places around the world. A 2010 report on the ten US cities with the largest per-capita Muslim populations contains names we might expect, like Detroit, New York, Houston, and Washington, DC. But it also contained a number of surprises, like Peoria, Illinois, and Cedar Rapids, Iowa.[1] When you consider specific Muslim ethnic groups, the results can be even more surprising. For example, in 2015,

Memphis, Tennessee, boasted the largest Kurdish population in the United States by far.

Or consider the mostly Hindu people from the Indian subcontinent. Yes, you will find them in places like New York or San Francisco. But you'll also find large populations in Dallas, Texas, and over thirty thousand Indians living in Phoenix, Arizona. Even Columbus, Ohio, and its surrounding area hosts around sixteen thousand recent immigrants from India.[2]

Many of us don't have to board international flights to reach people from other religions and cultures. We just need to open our eyes, look around, and engage the nations in our own cities and towns. Strangely, gospel work right here at home can seem more daunting than a two-week trip around the globe. Many people just don't know where to start, where to find unreached populations, or how to engage them with the gospel. But if we are spending good effort to see the gospel taken to places distant from us, it makes sense to notice the people that God has brought to our own doorsteps.

There isn't a magic recipe for how to encourage this in any given congregation. Where you are located, who lives around you, and what your congregation is like all influence how you might go about this. But we can think about a few useful principles and reflect on some of the experiences of one local church.

1. *Research.* A first step is to find out who from other cultures and ethnic groups live in your area. This is as simple as opening your eyes as you drive around different parts of your city. Are there a lot of "Halal" food markets in a part of town near you? Chances are you have Muslims neighbors.

Visiting ethnic grocery stores can be an especially good way to learn about and connect with specific ethnic or religious communities. These markets often have bulletin boards with information about events, festivals, and community needs that might provide opportunities to find out more and build relationships. Of course, just doing some straightforward on-line demographic research about your community can be easy and useful too.

2. *Take initiative.* Whatever you discover about your community, it will generally take initiative and encouragement to get your congregation engaged. In my local church we con-cluded that the main population of internationals in our vi-cinity was students. So we began to pray occasionally in our public prayer meetings that God would allow us to reach in-ternational students with the gospel.

Reliance on God in prayer, however, is not the enemy of human initiative. One of our elders took initiative too. He sat down with a fellow church member who had himself been converted as an international student from Singapore while in London. This young man began hosting a Bible study for international students to model and encourage this outreach. Over time it developed into English-language classes on two local university campuses and a network of church members meeting one-on-one with students interested in studying the Bible in English. Ultimately more than fifty church members were meeting each week to explore the Bible with students from countries where evangelism is severely restricted.

3. *Try different things.* What might that look like in your own congregation? It could mean hosting English classes at

your church, or members joining local adult soccer clubs dominated by internationals. Or connecting with efforts to resettle refugees, or volunteering to meet newly arriving international students at the airport. Each of these can be a great entry point. But the best way to reach out to internationals may just be your friendliness and openness when you bump into them in shops, on the street, or in your neighborhood.

4. *Talk to people.* One member of our church met a Muslim woman who'd begun working in the shop where she had her hair styled. During their very first meeting the Christian woman mentioned she was getting her hair done for a friend's wedding. Then she asked the Muslim woman—clearly new to our country—if she had ever been to a Christian wedding. She had not. So right then and there this Christian invited the woman to join her for the wedding at our church that weekend. The woman came, she heard the gospel, and a new friendship was born. It can be as easy as that.

5. *Practice international hospitality.* Most visitors and recent immigrants are naturally eager to meet locals and understand the local culture. Sadly, it's often reported that 80 percent of international students never see the inside of an American home during their stay. Long-term immigrants seem to fare only a little better. This is a great opportunity for Christians to exercise hospitality, and for you, as a church leader or member, to model this for others in your congregation. And that's true no matter what country you are in.

Holidays are especially good times to do this. Nearly every major holiday, our family has at least one or two international students join us for a meal. In the process, we are able to share with them our supreme thanks for the grace God has extended to us in Christ, as well as expose them to some pretty amusing food and cultural traditions.

6. *Prepare to be patient.* However you go about pursuing relationships with internationals, you should recognize some of the challenges involved. For starters, the time expectations of internationals can sometimes take Americans by surprise. Other cultures often have much greater time expectations for friendships. You need to be prepared and willing to educate your international friends about your culture by kindly setting boundaries that are appropriate for you and your family.

You'll also need a great deal of patience for long-term investment in relationships. Often a lot of underbrush needs to be cleared away before the gospel begins to take root. North American culture is far from Christian, but it does seem that many North Americans have some passing affinity for the gospel, whether through parents, relatives, or friends. And there is at least some cultural fluency with gospel ideas, even if twisted.

But for many of our friends from other cultures, there is none of that. They may have never known a Christian before and may have no affinity for the Bible or the gospel. Persons from Muslim or some Hindu communities may even have been taught to hate Christians and the Bible. Or your international friends may have come from a radically secular culture, as in much of China, where theistic belief is equated with mental deficiency. God can and will do whatever he pleases, but in the normal course of things, it usually takes a good bit of time and patience to work through the questions that these cultural hurdles create. But the fruit is worth the effort.

REACHING THE NATIONS THROUGH INTERNATIONAL EXPATRIATE CHURCHES

It was summer 2004 and I was traveling around a Muslim nation in Central Asia. With me was a young pastor and his wife. They felt a strong pull to take the gospel to the Muslim world. Mature and theologically solid folks, they seemed like the kind of people who could thrive in another culture. Yet as we traveled through a 99 percent Muslim nation, it became clear they wouldn't be heading here as missionaries.

The man felt compelled to preach, and he longed to shepherd a congregation. But in this nation, local opposition and government hostility meant that such preaching was out of the question. Instead, his role there would almost certainly be to evangelize and quietly train leaders who would themselves preach and pastor churches. By the end of our trip we were all pretty sure that pioneer church planting in a Muslim context was probably not for them. But that wasn't the end of the story.

Soon afterward a struggling English-language international church in an Arab Muslim nation contacted our church for help finding a new pastor. It seemed like a great match for this couple. The husband could preach and pastor a congregation of expats (foreigners), in English, yet could still work to evangelize and influence work among Muslims.

That was in 2005. Since then God has exceeded even our highest expectations. As that congregation has grown in health and diversity, it has become a doorway to the nations. Far from being a club for Westerners, the congregation is full of expat Arabs, Indians, and Filipinos. Their impact has been broad and deep. They've planted other churches nearby and in other cities. They've helped train local pastors from nearby Muslim nations and encouraged indigenous evangelism. This isn't exactly pioneer church planting. It might not even be missions in the most restrictive sense of the term. But encouraging these kinds of gospel outposts can be a wonderful tool for the gospel—especially in nations hostile to indigenous Christian witness.

Our own churches should also consider how to support efforts like this, not merely with money, but with the greater sacrificial gift of our people. We should help young men realize they don't always have to choose *either* to be pastors *or* to labor among the nations. Sometimes they can do both, even in some pretty restricted nations. We should also consider how we might send ordinary, faithful church members to join with and support churches like these (more on that in a moment).

But there are some special blessings and challenges that go along with this kind of work.

Blessings of International Expat Churches

1. *Supporting missionaries.* International churches can support and help more traditional, full-time missionaries who need encouragement, fellowship, and faithful teaching. This is especially true until new missionaries learn a local language and—if possible—join a local-language church, because they still need to obey Hebrews 10:25 and to assemble with a local church whenever possible. They still need a church commu-

nity in which to serve and be served. Who knows what ministries an international church may encourage simply through the missionaries it sustains, loves, disciples, and serves?

2. *Modeling biblical church health.* In addition, a healthy international church can be a great resource for other local pastors by modeling good preaching and biblical structures. There will be some cultural differences between international churches and indigenous churches, even in the same city. But if the Bible is really sufficient everywhere, the basics of preaching from the Bible and biblical church structures are right everywhere. The pattern of churches where members serve, rather than just look to be served, is needed everywhere. Especially in places where these biblical concepts have either not been taught or been poorly modeled by Western missionaries, the example of a biblical expat church can do much to undo that damage.

3. *Providing a platform for access, relationships, and training.* I'm frequently amazed at the countries that oppose missionary work but welcome English-language expat churches (or at least turn a blind eye to them). These churches can have a wonderful threefold utility in those contexts.

First, many godly business people wisely won't think of moving their families to a city without a gospel-preaching church. When one exists, living there becomes a possibility. Second, with those families come all sorts of relationships outside the church. Like any other church, the measure of an international expat church is not merely who comes through the door but also what doors are open to the members when they leave the church gathering. Finally, these churches can be hubs and platforms for serious Bible training. Because of their open, visible status, they can sometimes bring in others for training with minimal interference.

I know of one international church that regularly welcomes pastors from a heavily restricted nearby nation. There the pastors can get training, find encouragement, and observe a healthy congregation. Then they head back to their own country to pastor more faithfully beyond the reach of most Western passports.

Challenges of International Expat Churches

With all these blessings, there can also be special challenges in leading an international expatriate congregation.

1. *Leading a mixed community to unity.* The fact that only one or two expat churches might exist in a given city can create a tremendous pressure to minimize important doctrinal distinctives so that all God's children can gather together. But if you want to have a church that takes the Bible and its doctrines seriously, downplaying teaching just won't work.

For instance, you will need to teach that baptism is either for believers only or also for the children of church members. Where Jesus said, in Matthew 18:17, "Tell it to the church," you will either think he actually meant the congregation or believe he really meant the board of elders or a bishop in another town. But if there is only one international church in your town, you may feel great pressure to discount the Bible's teaching either way so that everyone can gather together in that one church.

The sad result of that good intention is often doctrinally

lowest-common-denominator churches that may unintentionally set an unbiblical example for local Christians. If you ever want to lead an expat church in another culture, it's likely this challenge will have to be dealt with.

2. *Shallow commitment.* Expat churches often have to contend with the shallow commitment of some who will seek to join. Nominal Christians who wouldn't bother to attend a church in their home country may want to join one overseas more for a sense of familiar community than out of love for Christ. This is both a great evangelistic opportunity and a great pastoral challenge.

3. *Legal pressures to exclude locals.* The greatest membership challenge may not be lukewarm expats but eager locals. In many places the government will allow expat churches on the implied (or stated) condition that the local population not be allowed to attend. Different international churches have dealt with this in different ways. Some reason that they should obey God rather than man and simply welcome all comers to attend, be baptized, and join. Others are more careful or shrewd, but still aim to make the gospel available to all. I fear that some, in cowardly unfaithfulness, decide to keep the gospel to themselves so as not to rock the boat. Whatever they decide, this can be one of the thorniest matters for such a church to navigate.

4. *Acts 6 all over again.* In even the best of international churches, where many different cultures are represented, the same cultural conflicts found in Acts 6 are likely. One cultural group may dominate, leaving another feeling undervalued or marginalized. Maintaining unity amid so much diversity will take great wisdom and a commitment to the Bible as

111

normative, rather than any particular cultural representation. Wisely sharing leadership among various ethnicities is a must.

5. *Cross-cultural stress.* Added to all this are the challenges members may face while living and potentially raising a family in another culture. This might be especially hard where participation in an expat church restricts immersion into the surrounding culture. It may mean feeling a step removed from the local population, or not learning the language as well as a traditional missionary would. All these may add to the challenges of this kind of cross-cultural living and ministry. Still, when done well, this kind of work is surely worth it.

Supporting International Expat Churches

How can our churches play a part in this ministry? First, we can encourage men training for pastoral ministry to consider pastoring a church overseas. We can consider whether our congregations could help support the establishment of new international churches. Some international churches don't intend for their own members to ever support the ministry from which they benefit (as Gal. 6:6 commands). This raises theological questions. But certainly these works ordinarily need start-up money. Though some Christians dislike meeting spaces that are purposely built to house churches, some countries expect or even require expats to build such meeting places; and supporting such projects may be a useful investment. More pastors ought to think about using their gifts in these kinds of churches. But this kind of service isn't only for pastors and preachers. Mature Christians can use their job skills to relocate and come alongside others in this gospel work. The possibilities are immense.

A good church is a good thing anywhere. And the best things about a good international church are common to every faithful church. God has committed himself to use gatherings of his people in every place to display the wisdom of his gospel plan to the watching world (Eph. 3:10). But there's a special kind of glory in a serious, gospel-centered church in a place otherwise devoid of gospel light. The darker the room, the brighter the candle's light. That's true even if the particular church isn't in the local language. Though not the same as churches taking root among the local population, it can still be a start, a help, and a glorious witness.

REACHING THE NATIONS THROUGH YOUR JOB

Workers Needed

Such international churches don't just need pastors and money. They need faithful members devoted to the fellowship and to reaching the peoples around them. As the world's economy becomes more global, many Christians have a renewed awareness of the role Christian migration and merchants have played in supporting the spread of the gospel. Starting with the refugees scattered by persecution in Acts 8:4, who were "preaching the word" as they went, Christians have helped to spread the gospel in the course of normal life, including travel or immigration. This New Testament pattern continued with traders on the Silk Road, merchants to India, laborers to South America, and modern employees of multinational companies. For centuries Christians have spread the gospel when other factors like employment have moved them around the world.

Most of us will work a job forty hours or so a week regardless of where we live. And most of us are going to meet our neighbors. We'll shop in the same places over and over and get to know folks who work there. Our children will make friends at school, and we'll get to know their parents. We'll have lunch with coworkers or clients. No matter where we live, our lives will have many of these same components. Imagine, then, if instead of doing those things where there might already be thousands of Christians, you did all this in a place where most people had never met a Christian or heard the gospel. What if you lived in a city that was 95 percent Muslim or 95 percent Hindu? What new gospel opportunities might that provide?

Yes, God the Holy Spirit has chosen to focus the church's effort on training, sending, and supporting missionaries sent out "for the sake of the name." Perhaps that's why the book of Acts gives only passing mention to the impact of Christian evangelism in the course of everyday travels and focuses almost exclusively on God's work through the apostles and other missionaries sent by churches. But just because an actor doesn't occupy the starring role on God's missionary stage doesn't mean he or she has no valuable part to play. Planting your life and career in a strategic place for the sake of the gospel among the nations may be a very good idea and a great support for global missions.

Pioneer Church-Planting Support

There will always be a need for supported missionaries sent out by obedient local churches. This is especially critical in pioneer areas where the press of learning a language in a new culture is a full-time pursuit in and of itself. But consider how pioneer missionaries could be helped if several families of mature Christians moved to their city to work normal jobs in order to help and encourage that missionary. One of the greatest needs of pioneer missionaries is spiritual encouragement. By definition they are in places with few, if any, other Christians.

What if mature Christians could covenant with those missionaries and gather with them as a church? What if they began to invite missionaries into the network of relationships afforded by their jobs? What if they could provide support, help with family needs, and even encourage new believers, if language allowed? Supplying this kind of fellowship and support would be hard and costly work, but it could provide life-changing help for pioneer missionaries. And yet, it would be a special kind of work, probably not a good fit for most working Christians.

Build on an Existing Foundation

A better plan for most Christians may be to join and support the work of an established expat church. As in their home country, an established church would provide the context and framework for their Christian life. Most of us need that kind of fellowship and framework to thrive as Christians. That's why Christ established his church and warns us never to forsake gathering with a local congregation (Heb. 10:25). Living overseas doesn't change this need or erase God's command. Certainly you need a church that uses a language you know well. For most, that would probably mean an expat church that speaks a language other than the local tongue.

If you were a part of a local congregation of expats hoping to be salt and light in its community, how might that multiply your own efforts? You might not have the time and opportunities a full-time missionary has, but not everyone is wired to be a full-time missionary. Still, most every Christian is wired to work, live, and love in the context of faithful membership in a local church. Isn't it worth considering the possibility of living that out in a place with fewer Christians?

CONCLUDING THOUGHTS

Whether we live in our home country or on the other side of the world, in full-time ministry or supporting ourselves with a job, God has laid the nations at our door. In many ways it has never been easier to personally engage other peoples with the gospel. May God give us boldness, wisdom, and creativity to think of ways to respond to his kindness, so that through us and our churches, even the distant islands can sing for joy (Isaiah 42).

CONCLUSION

Stepping toward the Nations

I began this book with a story about Beth and her dysfunctional church missions committee meeting. Perhaps you saw your own church reflected in some of the challenges in Beth's congregation. Your members may confuse good works with gospel missions, prize short-term trips mainly for their own personal enrichment, or always look for the next shortcut to make missions easy and fast. Maybe you are in a congregation where members are confused about what the mission of the church really is, how to do it, and whom the mission is for.

If the ideas in this short book seem wise and biblical, what remains is to plan your next steps. To help, let me summarize a few key points.

1. *Leaders need to lead.* It all starts with the leaders of your congregation. It's wonderful when an individual member or two gains a more biblical perspective on missions. But things will likely change for the better when leaders begin to lead in a more healthy direction. If you are a leader in your church, start leading. Teach the missionary implications of the gospel every time it comes up in the biblical text. Give out good

books on missions to the members of your church. Lead with determination, but also with gentleness and great patience. Introduce your congregation to faithful missionaries. Consider opportunities to travel overseas yourself to support their work. Often nothing speaks more loudly to a congregation about the importance of missions and the value of specific missionaries than for a pastor to invest his own time and energies.

2. *Every member can help.* Even if you are a church member without any formal leadership role, you can still work to encourage your congregation in missions. But you need to be careful. Before anything else, talk to your pastor, elders, or missions leader. Perhaps give him your copy of this book to read before you talk. Work patiently and wisely. We never want to let Satan use our enthusiasm for even good things as something that undermines a church's unity. Take your time, and make sure the leaders of your congregation are with you. And by all means, pray. Ask God to help your congregation gain a bigger, more biblical view of global missions. He's a good God, and he loves to answer prayers to help his churches.

3. *Teach for a biblical worldview.* The best way to change how a church does missions is not by decree but by teaching. Work to change the worldview of your congregation, first by making sure that the gospel is clearly understood and loved by your members. Then work on their worldview for missions. Talk about the special mission of the church to guard the gospel and to proclaim it to all peoples. Help members understand the role of church planting. Teach them about God's control of all things and his faithfulness. A good understanding of God's decisive role in salvation is the best foundation to help

a church discern between faithful and unfaithful approaches to missions.

4. *Invest in long-term relationships.* Begin to invest in long-term relationships overseas with people you trust and respect. Through your existing network of churches, ask about faithful ministries or missionaries they support, and look for ways to encourage and help them in their work. Invite some faithful missionaries to spend extended time with your congregation. Or pay them a visit to help with a project or just get to know their work. Be patient. Build slowly and faithfully, yet urgently.

5. *Resist the lure of immediate results.* As you invest in long-term relationships and evaluate work, resist the siren call of immediate visible results. Think carefully about how you evaluate workers you support. Base your evaluation on relationships that allow you to know the faithfulness and wisdom of those you support. Where those elements are present, persevere. Encourage workers who toil in fields with hard soil. Keep praying for them and with them. Remember, they are longing for visible fruit, for converts, for churches, and for Christ to be glorified in their cities. Don't add to that pressure by telling them you expect to see large numbers. As you spend your money, don't just send it to groups that boast the most impressive-sounding results. Get to know workers and ministries, look for gospel faithfulness, and then get behind them in as big a way as you can.

6. *Rely on urgent confidence.* Finally, as we engage and labor in the work of missions, we need an urgent confidence. We should have urgency because sin is real and hell is bad, and

confidence because God is so good and heaven so glorious. Why dawdle on the way to the victory celebration?

We should have confidence because we know the mission will not fail. We may fail in our faithfulness, but God will not fail in his mission. Christ *will* have the nations for his inheritance. Frantic speculation and guilt are weak motivators compared with the truth of God's unstoppable plan to rescue every child for whom Christ died. Christ will not lose any of those whom the Father has given him, and God has chosen to use us—in countless local churches—as the agents of his gospel triumph.

NOTES

Epilogue

1. J. H. Bavinck, *An Introduction to the Science of Missions* (Philadelphia: Presbyterian and Reformed, 1960), 5.

Foreword

1. George F. Pentecost, quoted in John M. Moore, "The Presentation of Missions from the Pulpit," *Missions* 6, nos. 7–8 (1915): 613.

Chapter 1: A Biblical Foundation for Missions

1. John Piper, Twitter post, January 23, 2011 (1:00 p.m.), https://twitter.com/JohnPiper.

2. For example, Robert D. Putnam, "What's So Darned Special about Church Friends?," *Altruism, Morality and Social Solidarity Forum* (American Sociological Association) 3, no. 2 (2012): 1, 19–21.

3. Robert Woodberry, "The Missionary Roots of Liberal Democracy," *American Political Science Review* 106, no. 2 (2012): 244–74.

Chapter 2: First Things First

1. Stephen Neill, *Creative Tension* (London: Edinburgh House, 1959), 81.

Chapter 4: Getting the House in Order

1. Charles Bridges, *The Christian Ministry* (London: Banner of Truth: 1958), 75.

Chapter 5: Healthy Missions Partnerships

1. This chapter is partially adapted from an article previously published by 9Marks: Andy Johnson, "Missions Partnerships from the Home Church's Perspective," *9Marks*, February 26, 2010,

https://9marks.org/article/missions-partnerships-home-churchs
-perspective/.

2. Bill Turpie, ed., *Ten Great Preachers: Messages and Interviews* (Grand Rapids, MI: Baker, 2000), 117.

Chapter 6: Reforming Short-Term Missions

1. Don Fanning, "Short Term Missions: A Trend That Is Growing Exponentially," *Trends and Issues in Missions* 4 (2009), http://digital commons.liberty.edu/cgm_missions/4. Fanning reports that short-term missions has grown about 8000 percent since 1980—from twenty thousand to 1.6 million. Long-term missions grew by about 10 percent during the same period.

2. Downers Grove, IL: InterVarsity Press, 2000.

Chapter 7: Engaging the Nations by Other Means

1. Kate Shellnutt, "Houston among the Top 10 Muslim Cities in U.S.," *Houston Chronicle*, August 12, 2010, accessed September 6, 2016, http://blog.chron.com/believeitornot/2010/08/houston -among-the-top-10-muslim-cities-in-u-s/.

2. "Total U.S. Indian American Population," Pew Research Center, www.pewsocialtrends.org/asianamericans-maps/#indian.

GENERAL INDEX

missions agencies, 50–52
"Missions Reading Group," 47–48
money, trustworthiness with, 43
multinational corporations, 114
Muslims
    evangelism of, 70–71
    in the United States, 102–3, 105, 106

nations, at our doorstep, 102, 116
Neill, Stephen, 35
numbers, in missions, 68–69

parachurch organizations, 27, 44, 51
partnerships, 57, 75–86
passion, to see Christ glorified, 40, 47
pastor, leadership in missions, 79–81
pastoral visits, with missionaries, 53–54, 60
patience
    with internationals, 106
    in missions, 69
    in short-term missions, 98
Paul
    and church in Antioch, 14–15, 88
    missionary journeys of, 88–89
    as pioneer church planter, 62–63
    on relationships, 55
peace with God, 34
Pentecost, George, 13
personal theology, 65
pietism, 49
pioneer church planting, 62–64, 115
Piper, John, 22
pragmatism, 78
prayer, 80, 84, 104
preaching, 79
provincialism, 80
Putnam, Robert, 23

relationships, 60, 62, 68, 81–82, 86
research, 103–4
results, lure of, 68, 71, 119

sending agencies, 50–52
servant-mindedness, 77–79
service, of short-term missions, 97
short-term missions, 18, 55–56, 78–79, 82
    cost of, 91–92
    goal of, 92
    and long-term view, 93–95
    low maintenance, 97–98
    reforming of, 87–99
    as support for long-term partners, 84–85
Silk Road, 113
social action, 22
social media, 48
stewardship, 22, 42
Stott, John, 80
strengthening churches, 61, 62, 64
syncretism, 45

teammates, 56–57
theological training, of missionaries, 45
trust, 70, 75–76, 85

unreached, 62–63
urgency in missions, 68

weariness, in short-term missions, 96
Woodberry, Robert, 23
world travelers, 48
worldview for missions, 118
wrath of God, 22, 33

zeal vs. foolishness, 59

SCRIPTURE INDEX

a division of 10ofthose.com

10Publishing is the publishing house of **10ofThose**.
It is committed to producing quality Christian resources that
are biblical and accessible.

www.10ofthose.com is our online retail arm selling thousands
of quality books at discounted prices.

For information contact: **info@10ofthose.com**
or check out our website: **www.10ofthose.com**